NEW DIRECTIONS FOR HIGHER

Martin Kramer
EDITOR-IN-CHIEF

Reconceptualizing the Collegiate Ideal

J. Douglas Toma
University of Missouri-Kansas City

Adrianna J. Kezar
George Washington University

EDITORS

Number 105, Spring 1999

JOSSEY-BASS PUBLISHERS
San Francisco

RECONCEPTUALIZING THE COLLEGIATE IDEAL
J. Douglas Toma, Adrianna Kezar (eds.)
New Directions for Higher Education, no. 105
Volume XXVII, Number 1
Martin Kramer, Editor-in-Chief

ISSN 0271–0560   ISBN 0–7879–4857–8

NEW DIRECTIONS FOR HIGHER EDUCATION is part of The Jossey-Bass Higher and Adult Education Series and is published quarterly by Jossey-Bass Inc., Publishers, 350 Sansome Street, San Francisco, California 94104–1342. Periodicals postage paid at San Francisco, California, and at additional mailing offices. Postmaster: Send address changes to New Directions for Higher Education, Jossey-Bass Inc., Publishers, 350 Sansome Street, San Francisco, California 94104–1342.

SUBSCRIPTIONS cost $56.00 for individuals and $99.00 for institutions, agencies, and libraries. See Ordering Information page at end of book.

EDITORIAL CORRESPONDENCE should be sent to the Editor-in-Chief, Martin Kramer, 2807 Shasta Road, Berkeley, California 94104–1342.

Cover photograph and random dot by Richard Blair/Color & Light © 1990.

Jossey-Bass Web address: www.josseybass.com

CONTENTS

EDITORS' NOTES   1
J. Douglas Toma, Adrianna J. Kezar

1. Transformations of the American College Ideal: Six Historic   7
Ways of Learning
Lester F. Goodchild
There are six historic ways of learning in American education. These pro-
vide a framework for understanding the American collegiate ideal, but a
comprehensive vision of that ideal for the future is still lacking.

2. The Diverse Campus: Broadening Our Ideal to Incorporate   25
All Voices
Adrianna J. Kezar
The collegiate ideal, often associated with elitism in higher education, has
changed over time to become more pluralistic and thus to more accurately
reflect increasingly diverse student populations.

3. Developing the Whole Student: The Collegiate Ideal   35
Lisa E. Wolf-Wendel, Marti Ruel
Because traditional models for developing the "whole student" no longer
serve the diverse populations of students increasingly pursuing higher education, a new philosophy focusing on the partnership between student
affairs professionals and faculty members is necessary to further student
development goals.

4. The Student Affairs Establishment and the Institutionalization   47
of the Collegiate Ideal
Anna M. Ortiz
Through their structure and services, student affairs units have institutionalized the collegiate ideal on many campuses. In order for the collegiate ideal
to evolve to represent and encourage a more inclusive environment, student
affairs professionals must examine their policies and procedures and make
changes needed to meet the developmental needs of non-traditional students.

5. Faculty Culture and College Life: Reshaping Incentives Toward   59
Student Outcomes
Marilyn J. Amey
At many research universities, faculty incentives have moved further from
student needs. Is it inevitable that research-oriented faculty divorce themselves from campus life, and are there ways to reshape the incentive system—to incorporate faculty contributions to their own institutions,
especially in regard to student development?

6. Challenges Facing Shared Governance Within the College 71
Christopher C. Morphew
How might technological and environmental changes reshape the model of shared governance between faculty and administrators in higher education that plays such a vital role in our conception of the collegiate ideal?

7. The Collegiate Ideal and the Tools of External Relations: 81
The Uses of High-Profile Intercollegiate Athletics
J. Douglas Toma
High-profile athletic programs provide a powerful tool to connect external constituents and campus communities alike with the collegiate traditions that form the essence of institutional culture at large universities.

8. Vocational Education and the Collegiate Ideal: The Threat and 91
the Challenge of Limited Resources
Linda Serra Hagedorn
Although fiscal restraints have had an impact upon all levels of postsecondary education, community college vocational programs have been particularly hard hit. An examination of present conditions provides an approach toward a realistic "ideal."

9. Redefining Campus: Urban Universities and the Idea of Place 101
Erin McNamara Horvat, Kathleen M. Shaw
University-community partnerships at urban universities offer an important illustration of the idea of "place" in higher education.

10. The Collegiate Ideal in the Twenty-First Century 109
Arthur W. Chickering, Jackson Kytle
The colleges of the twenty-first century must incorporate the educational fundamentals underlying traditional residential institutions, no matter what form these fundamentals might take.

INDEX 121

EDITORS' NOTES

Our uniquely American conception of higher education has long been intertwined with the notion of college. Over time, institutions evolved into different types, (e.g, research universities, community colleges), as they responded to societal needs. These new institutional forms broadened access and mission, yet they never lost the ideals of Oxford and Cambridge that shaped early colleges. Although increasingly fewer of the aggregate number of students enrolled in post-secondary education have a traditional collegiate experience, the idea of the college or university as campus—an actual place where academic life and community life assume something approaching equal importance—retains a favored status. Indeed, the notion of place is the core of our traditional attachment to alma mater that so distinguishes the American model of higher education. But tension is developing as new demands for broader access and mission are being sorted out at the end of the millennium.

As access to higher education continues to increase, however, does the collegiate ideal necessarily become unworkable? Thus far, campuses have been able to graft some portion of collegiate life onto the new forms of post-secondary education that have emerged—the research university, the urban university, the community college. If higher education becomes increasingly less about place as technology assumes a greater role in the delivery of education, does our traditional notion of community at colleges and universities retain a role? Similarly, as higher education increasingly focuses on training and retraining increasing numbers of older and returning students, does campus life become irrelevant or impractical?

To portray the collegiate ideal as a dated cultural artifact—an elitist and romanticized vision of the university that is contrary to expanding access and scope—is to understate its history and current utility. Student development theorists argue persuasively that learning involves interactions between students and between student and faculty, particularly when the actors involved carry different cultural perspectives. Current initiatives to educate the whole person are a continuation of the traditional role assumed by colleges and universities in training citizen-leaders for society. Much of this interaction and training takes place in activities and organizations outside of the classroom. The idea of the active campus also benefits other stakeholders in the university. It is the basis of much of the alumni and community attachment to the institution that is so essential in attracting external support. The active campus makes colleges and universities more attractive to students who have long had a multitude of enrollment options. Finally, it provides faculty and staff with a sense of community that encourages loyalty and productivity.

The traditional idea of college will likely persist for those who can afford to spend the customary four years on a residential campus. These students will continue to reap the increase in learning outcomes as well as the cultural capital associated with the campus environment. Still, in a democratic society, the genius of the collegiate ideal is that it has been available to all types of students. Students at different types of institutions experience their campuses in different manners, but they still experience them as places and as encounters with people.

Many questions remain unanswered: If higher education evolves to have ever less to do with the idea of place, do we risk what has made American higher education both so distinctive and successful? Is the collegiate ideal in danger of becoming an anachronism as higher education expands the access that has always been part of its history? Or, does a redefinition of the collegiate ideal which incorporates diverse students and diverse pedagogies present exciting opportunities to enhance the quality of student experience and lifelong personal development for everyone? These are the questions we explore throughout the chapters of this issue offering varying perspectives about current challenges and future prospects. Goodchild begins the discussion with the challenge of defining the collegiate ideal in the twenty-first century. In the final chapter, Chickering and Kytle expand on the notions described throughout the earlier chapters and begin to define the new vision. Since the vision is still being shaped, we hope you will become engaged in this struggle, adding your own insights.

Our discussion begins with Goodchild, who traces six conceptions of the American Collegiate ideal: the colonial way, frontier way, collegiate way, town way, community way, and distance way. These different ideal conceptions illustrate that notions about American higher education have changed over the years and that what is considered the best way to educate is constantly changing. Yet, at the same time there are certain principles that have remained constant, such as educating the whole person, collegial decision-making, affiliation with the institution, community, relationships, and diverse purposes.

As a new vision for the collegiate ideal in the twenty-first century evolves, it is important to consider and learn from earlier notions. It is important to build on our distinguished past, since American higher education has long been unparalleled worldwide. Is the collegiate ideal something that has changed as institutions have evolved to incorporate increasing numbers of people of color, women, the disabled, and non-traditional aged students, or does it remain, fundamentally, an elite and exclusive white male construct? Has the collegiate ideal adapted to changes? Kezar explores whether the collegiate ideal can serve a more diverse student body. She reviews the research on women and students of color within traditional college and university structures, examining whether these characteristics have positive outcomes for these students. The research overwhelmingly illustrates that the collegiate model has positive benefits for more diverse students. Several recent changes in the collegiate environment provide a direction for modifying structures and cultures to be even more positive for a diverse student body, including collaborative learning, community service learning, and learning communities.

Building on the concepts introduced in the chapter by Kezar, Wolf-Wendel, and Ruel remind us that with new students with more complex and diverse needs, the vision for the collegiate ideal must be expanded. The power of assessment to better understand the needs of students in the twenty-first century is noted as a tool for meeting this challenge. They also remind us that certain principles from the collegiate ideal, such as high expectations and letting students know they matter, will continue to be important. Wolf-Wendel and Ruel make an important argument and provide a challenge for the twenty-first century: "We have invested too much energy in chasing the ideal college student and not enough energy creating the ideal college."

The collegiate ideal has persisted, in large part, because it has become institutionalized through the student affairs bureaucracies that emerged early in the 20th century and have steadily grown throughout the century. Institutions have recognized the benefits of student life in attracting students to campus and retaining them once there. Accordingly, they have consciously attempted to develop in students a sense of identity with the institution that goes beyond their classroom encounters. Ortiz describes the collegiate ideal as a culture that can be helpful to students but that has disadvantages for non-traditional students as currently constructed. She urges student affairs divisions to transform their services and programs to make the benefits of the collegiate ideal available for all students. In Ortiz's chapter, the collegiate ideal can be seen as a more sinister culture, reminding us that it can and will have a negative impact on students if the image becomes reified and no longer evolves.

Amey explores a major force that affects the collegiate ideal: faculty reward systems. Particularly at the research universities that serve so many of the students enrolled in American higher education, faculty incentives are skewed away from the collegiate ideal. The notion of developing campus community has become the responsibility of the student affairs community and others in non-academic roles on campus. Is it inevitable that research-oriented faculty divorce themselves from campus life? This chapter discusses ways to reshape the incentive system for faculty to recognize their contributions as campus citizens, particularly in endeavors that relate to student development. Is this something that we want to do, or are there adequate surrogates for faculty involvement? Amey's chapter highlights conversations happening nationally that attempt to reshape structures and cultures that operate to stifle learning and take away from the collegiate mission. These revolve around a focus on learning, assessment, learning communities, on-line communities, and the changing role of faculty.

Morphew reminds us that the collegiate ideal is shaped by larger governance patterns and forces outside the institution. The author reminds us that shared governance is a tradition that has shaped the collegiate environment for hundreds of years. He warns that attempts to modify this long standing tradition should be examined with strict scrutiny. Rapid expansion of part-time faculty and the pressure to contain costs while providing more services and programs significantly affect the environment in which the collegiate ideal unfolds. Often these choices are being made without reference to their impact on the traditional environment that has proven successful.

Institutions make a concentrated effort to reach out to external constituents—alumni, potential donors, legislators—and often use the campus life at the core of the collegiate ideal as a hook. Toma examines one of the significant features of the collegiate ideal—athletics—and illuminates the way it shapes our notions about college life. Does this model continue to make sense as higher education changes? Does it suggest that the collegiate ideal applies only to elite higher education or is it possible to connect other types of college experiences to something that goes beyond the classroom? In essence, what are the uses of the collegiate ideal in areas outside of student development? This chapter extends the collegiate ideal beyond its impact on students to the community and to society at large. For some individuals, college athletics is their first or only exposure to the college experience or collegiate way. It is through sports that campuses extend their influence to the broader society, drawing support and resources. Toma reminds us that moving away from traditional collegiate life could mean the loss of valuable aspects of the campus, such as sports, that provide broad-reaching support for colleges and universities.

Hagedorn shows us that the collegiate ideal is not just something reserved for colleges or universities, but that vocational and community colleges also mirror many aspects of the collegiate way. However, reduced funding threatens to damage the type and quality of education provided. In particular, technical education depends on students working together with state-of-the-art equipment. This serves a socializing function—an apprenticeship model—that might not be possible through technology. This chapter also illustrates the impact of reduced funding on the quality of education. Leaders in higher education should realize that funding decisions have profound impacts on structures and cultures that have proven successful.

Horvat and Shaw illustrate that the urban university sector is another example of how the collegiate ideal has been modified to meet current realities and changing societal needs. The authors also describe how the urban sector can help us to develop a collegiate ideal for the twenty-first century built on a mission that is "part of" rather than "separated from" society. The traditional image of the college is the pastoral model, on a hilltop, in the countryside separated from the corruption of the city and real world. The authors argue that urban universities incorporate peer interaction and out-of-classroom learning without separating the student from community and society. One pedagogical tool offered, community service learning, can be used by faculty to expand the collegiate ideal to embrace society and the challenges it faces.

Lastly, Chickering and Kytle summarize the challenges facing higher education institutions brought about by changes in various aspects of the collegiate ideal: new student characteristics, complex societal needs, cost and accountability, new technologies, and unclear purpose. Chickering's and Kytle's summary provides a context for developing a vision for the collegiate ideal for the twenty-first century. Earlier chapters described various aspects of this new vision, but in this chapter the authors summarize how institutions can respond to the current challenges. The new vision for the collegiate ideal in the twenty-first century is institutions, with clear purposes, that maximize human inter-actions, utilize active and experiential pedagogies, recognize individual differ-ence, and set high expectations.

Certain themes emerge within each chapter: (1) research on involvement theory and informal learning outside the classroom provides support for the importance of the collegiate model; (2) benefits of the collegiate ideal for stu-dents, the campus community, and society as a justification for this model; (3) past evolution of the collegiate ideal provides a foundation for future change; (4) assessment as critical to evolution; (5) evolution of roles, structures, and cultures as necessary to meet current challenges; and, (6) current challenges such as technology or financial constraints are highlighted.

Chickering and Kytle summarize the research mentioned throughout the issue by chapter authors: illustrating the benefits of living on campus, being involved in out-of-classroom activities, peer interaction, and faculty and student contact. Almost every author discusses Kuh's and Whitt's *Involving Colleges* or Astin's *Involvement Theory*. This research can be used to build the model colle-giate ideal for the twenty-first century. Almost every author describes the ben-efits of the collegiate ideal for students. For example, Ortiz describes retention, improved grades, affiliation, and improved self-esteem to name a few. Kezar notes how students have improved learning outcomes and Wolf-Wendel and Ruel explain that a broader set of learning outcomes are developed within a col-legiate model. Toma describes the benefits of the collegiate ideal for the com-munity through athletic programs that provide entertainment, community spirit, and affiliation.

The notion of evolution is critical to various authors' discussions. Almost every author notes how the key to reaping the benefits of the collegiate ideal is the notion that colleges continually evolve and need to be re-examined. Assess-ment emerges as an important principle within several chapters. How can the collegiate ideal evolve without an understanding of its current state and the forces that are operating within and upon it? The evolution of roles, structures, and cultures is noted by most authors as important in developing the new ideal. Amey describes changing faculty roles, Ortiz suggests changing student affairs divisions, and Kezar reviews modified curricular structures such as learning communities. Each author reminds us that the collegiate ideal evolves not merely because of internal demands, but due to outside environmental changes, for example, demographic changes, and changes in governance structures.

Several authors describe challenges to the collegiate ideal. The diversity of students has complicated the notion of the collegiate ideal. Wolf-Wendel and Ruel, Kezar, and Ortiz all provide information to expand the collegiate ideal so that it meets the needs of diverse students. Other authors describe the oppor-tunities and promise of new conditions and challenges. For example, many authors see technology as a critical component within the new collegiate ideal. Amey discusses on-line communities, Chickering and Kytle describe the power of new technologies in active learning, and Goodchild describes the "distance way," a new collegiate model.

The various authors collectively agree that the collegiate ideal has strong potential in the next century as long as it continues to evolve. As each author in this volume suggests, the collegiate ideal has evolved significantly in the last forty years, yet at times this evolution has been slow. This volume does not definitively answer the question of whether the idea of the campus "as place" has become an anachronism. It does provide a detailed and thoughtful framework for examining this question, one that does not exist within the current debate. We hope that it will provide ideas for those making decisions about the future state of higher education. We hope that you will join us in the challenge of redefining the collegiate ideal in the twenty-first century.

J. Douglas Toma
Adrianna J. Kezar
Editors

J. DOUGLAS TOMA *is assistant professor of higher education at the University of Missouri-Kansas City and visiting assistant professor and senior research fellow at the Graduate School of Education and Institute for Research on Higher Education at the University of Pennsylvania.*

ADRIANNA J. KEZAR *is assistant professor of higher education at George Washington University and director of the ERIC Clearinghouse on Higher Education.*

Six historic ways of learning provide a framework for understanding the American collegiate ideal. A comprehensive vision of the collegiate ideal for the twenty-first century is still lacking.

Transformations of the American College Ideal: Six Historic Ways of Learning

Lester F. Goodchild

Alexander Meiklejohn, one of the most enlightened spokespersons for the American college ideal during this century, called a college "a place, a group, a comradeship of those who follow learning as their guide and who welcome others in the same pursuit." A college, he wrote, is a "spirit, a way of life, a manner of being. If it be the purpose of a college to follow after learning, whether it be science or philosophy, literature or art, no man is of the college who has ceased from that pursuit." For him, the college was a place of learning, a campus of mind: its purpose was "to start men on the way to learning" (1969, pp. 67, 70). Since 1912, Meiklejohn had held the presidency of Amherst College and was determined to address the twenty year barrage of criticism lobbed at the college. Meiklejohn believed that a liberal education was a means of "making minds"—a title he originally preferred for this work and only reluctantly changed in response to editorial demand. During the early 1930s, he created the famous Experimental College at the University of Wisconsin, putting his cherished ideals to the test. Meiklejohn designed a two-year liberal arts coherent curriculum which explored both Greek and American civilizations in hopes of cultivating intelligence through this study. A central feature of this residential college effort centered on an assessment of "the whole body of influences which play upon the undergraduate student" (Meiklejohn, 1932, xiii, xvi). This glimpse of Meiklejohn's collegiate ideal offers three characteristics of its larger American genus: the place itself, the central role of learning, and a comprehensive view of the collegiate environment. Embracing this insight, the collegiate ideal thus means

NEW DIRECTIONS FOR HIGHER EDUCATION, no. 105, Spring 1999 © Jossey-Bass Publishers an undergraduate's gradual adoption of a spirit of learning through some formal experience that becomes a way of life. In many ways, this scholar educator presaged the current concerns related to undergraduate education and assessment (Goodchild, 1997).

Yet what is the purpose of the American college? How did the collegiate ideal come about? What forces caused it to change? What importance does it have for understanding the development of American higher education? What meaning does it have for contemporary men's and women's multicultural undergraduate life? Following insights from Lawrence A. Cremin's intellectual history of education in his work, *The Transformation of the School: Progressivism in American Education, 1876–1957* (1961), this chapter explores the transformations of the collegiate ideal by offering a new interpretation of the history of the American college. This analysis employs an intellectual history perspective, but frames it within a larger geographic context. Central to this revisionist historiographic lens is the campus as a physical place and way of life. By using a more contextual geographic perspective to understand the development of the college, this interpretation accentuates the dynamics of historic societal expansion in North America. The college represented an important landmark in the establishment of a town or a city (Meinig, 1993). This insight reflects the now classic interpretation of David B. Potts's "'College Enthusiasm!' As Public Response, 1800–1860" (1977) and the earlier work of Daniel J. Boorstin on the "booster college" in *The Americans: The National Experience* (1965). Can this type of perspective be used in various eras? Such an attempt is greatly aided by D. W. Meinig's multivolume work, *The Shaping of America* (1986, 1993), published by Yale University Press.

Interpretive Historical Considerations

Employing a geographic and an intellectual historical perspective to describe the rise of the college ideal requires a short discussion of the contextual and conceptual framework for this analysis. In his second volume, *Continental America, 1800–1867* (1993), Meinig explores the expansion of the continental United States through a development of its geographic structure. He found Daniel J. Elazar's (1966, 1970) concept of the "geology of settlement" helpful in describing "the expansion from several regional societies of Atlantic America" westward. As "major streams of migration" emanated from New England, greater Pennsylvania, and greater Virginia after the American Revolution, these extended societies created villages, towns, and cities sequentially along the way (Meinig, 1993, p. 224).

These migrations followed various routes of travel whether they constituted wagon train trails, roads, rivers, canals, turnpikes, or railroads. These (what may be called) waves of extension provided the avenues for societal development. Meinig further found Malcolm Rohrbough's (1968) concepts of "pulsations (reflecting primarily the booms and busts of a volatile national economy) and broader phases (reflecting more basic changes in human geography and technology)" valuable in characterizing the development of this westward expansion.

The first of these phases began in the 1790s as an array of land tracts was put on the market in western New York, Pennsylvania, and the Ohio Valley, and the first of the federal lands in Ohio were surveyed and made available. Meanwhile, settlement in Kentucky and Tennessee was spreading outward from prospering nuclei in the Bluegrass and Nashville basins. Farther south a still experimental emphasis on cotton was generating strong pressures from several older districts. In all of these areas this was a time of difficult pioneering, suffering from meager facilities, chronic commercial instabilities, geopolitical uncertainties, and mounting fears about Indian retaliations. The war initiated in 1812 marked a tumultuous transition into a new phase (Meinig, 1993).

Revising the Turnerian concept of the frontier, Meinig showed how such pioneering resulted in the development of towns, thus creating an American system of regional development. He further followed Richard Wade's (1959) insightful realization that the town was "the spearhead of the frontier." The symbol of regional development became the instant town mushrooming on the frontier even before much of the forest had been felled or fields cleared in the countryside. Less romantic to a later age than the log cabin, the town was far more potent in the shaping of the nation. It represented an intense investment of energy and capital from the East to transform new outlying districts into fully integrated parts of the whole (Meinig, 1993).

In this developmental pattern, Native American society was transplanted sequentially by imperial, mercantile, and speculative frontiers as the army, farmers, and land speculators, respectively, established town and county infrastructures (Meinig, 1993). When churches and missionary societies began to serve these frontier societies, they sought to offer education. With the subsequent growth and consolidation of these areas, these groups established academies and colleges. Town "boosterism" (Boorstin, 1965; Potts, 1977) thus provided the enthusiasm for not only the development of the frontier but also the creation of institutions of higher learning. This geographic historical approach thus offers a new lens to examine the development of college establishment. A complementary intellectual historical lens for analyzing the development of the collegiate ideal comes from Frederick Rudolph's *The American College and University* (1962). His important interpretive chapter on "the collegiate way" describes the embodiment of the collegiate ideal as a residential way of life.

> The collegiate way is the notion that a curriculum, a library, a faculty, and students are not enough to make a college. It is an adherence to the residential scheme of things. It is respectful of quiet rural settings, dependent on dormitories, committed to dining halls, permeated by paternalism. It is what every American college has had or consciously rejected or lost or sought to recapture. It is William Tecumseh Sherman promising to be a father to an entire student body; it is comfort and full

tobacco jars in a Princeton dormitory; in an urban university it is counselors helping the socially inept to overcome their weaknesses [p.87].

The collegiate way was thus a way of life according to the residential college tradition where learning occurred through every aspect of campus life.
Yet, in his last application, Rudolph alludes to this concept being used for
higher education settings other than just the residential college. What other
"ways" of college life might there be? This chapter posits that there were other
ways related to the evolving mission and purpose of American higher education. In fact, the collegiate way represented only one of the various ways of life
in which a distinctive comprehensive setting devoted to higher education or a
mental attitude focused on higher learning might be normatively typed. Each
represented a particular worldview about the appropriate way college education could occur. By operationalizing the collegiate ideal in this fashion, it may
be perceived that these ideal ways apply to a formalized exchange of higher
learning wherever it might take place. This interpretation thus follows Meiklejohn's concept of "making minds" by reconceptualizing the collegiate ideal
as a campus of mind where undergraduate learners embrace a new intellectual
perspective. In the hagiography of American higher education, President James
A. Garfield's musings about the glories of nineteenth century learning to
Williams College alumni in 1871 best epitomizes this collegiate ideal: "Give
me a log hut with only a simple bench, Mark Hopkins on one end and I on the
other, and you may have all the buildings, apparatus, and libraries without
him" (Reinert, 1970, p. 145).

The purpose of this chapter then is to explore a geographic and an intellectual history of this revised collegiate ideal. From this point of view, the
American college went through six transformations of this ideal through its
history up to the present: (1) the colonial way, (2) the frontier way, (3) the collegiate way, (4) the town way, (5) the community way, and (6) the distance way.
Such a revisionist interpretation seeks to expand Rudolph's concept by apply-
ing it to the various stages of the development of the American college's mission and purpose, as phases of regional development enabled college
foundings to occur across the country and even now in cyberspace. It suggests
a sociological theory of academic institutional horizontal dispersion and vertical differentiation. It thus recasts the older idea of institutional aspiration
through which institutional administrations sought to move their colleges to
university stature in two ways. First, this theory posits that academic institutional dispersion occurred horizontally as college foundings followed waves of
migration extension that spread across the frontier along various travel routes.
As these institutions advanced, they further defined their institutional characters (Goodchild, 1986; Martin, 1982), often as a result of organizational sagas
(Clark, 1970). Second, depending upon the desires and determination of
administrators and trustees at some of these schools, they also decided to shift
their missions vertically from college to university status, while maintaining
their now undergraduate college. On the other hand, some disestablished their

mission, in unusual cases, to assume junior college status (for example, Vincennes University [Lawlis, 1982]). Such institutional differentiation often provided the means to revitalize the campus setting by adding professional or graduate education. These actions did much to weaken or strengthen evolving institutional collegiate characters. This new interpretation begins by analyzing the Puritan founding of Harvard College.

The Six Ways of the American Collegiate Ideal

The American collegiate ideal has six ways: the colonial way, the frontier way, the collegiate way, the town way, the community way, and the distance way.

The Colonial Way. Puritan colonization brought approximately 20,000 pioneers to North American shores between 1630 and 1660 alone. This New England society sought to establish settlements and towns to recreate an enlightened Protestant community. Welcomed by the Native American Pequot, Narragansett, and Wampanoag tribes, who were relatively few in number, the Puritans experienced rapid development. They established fourteen Indian mission villages where Puritan ministers taught Western language, ideas, and religion. Such tribal accommodations ended when these societies stood estranged by the time of King Philip's War in 1675. During this tragedy, close to one thousand English and some three thousand Indians died (Meinig, 1986). With acquisition of more lands through later colonial extensions, Puritans determined to establish their cultural way of life with the education of their children in schools and a college. It became the "New England Way" (Staloff, 1998).

In his classic, *The New England Mind: The Seventeenth Century* (1939), Perry Miller described a seventeenth century theocratic worldview which enlivened this colonial Puritan community. Its furtherance rested greatly upon the creation of a college. In 1636, Harvard's overseers proclaimed that the institution "was to advance Learning and perpetuate it to Posterity" (p. 75). Yet what determined its purpose? Scholarly opinions have varied over the primary theological or liberal orientation of its institutional mission: Was it a seminary for theological studies or a college for liberal learning? The fact that fifty percent of its graduates went on to the ministry before the Revolution argued strongly for a theological orientation. On the other hand, the rest of the graduates assumed leading positions in the colony or in trade. A more recent assessment opts for both interpretations (Bailyn, 1986). Nevertheless, the institution breathed a theological metaphysics, infusing all aspects of collegiate instruction and life with Christian Puritan ideas. Initially, the site of this institution offered protection from the heterodox sentiment brewing in Boston, as determined by the colonial General Court. Newtown, now called Cambridge, provided a place where Pastor Thomas Shepard had evangelized the population so that the town was "kept spotless from the contagion" (Morison, 1935, pp. 182–183). Because the communal goal in erecting this college was to create both "a learned clergy and a lettered people" (Rudolph, 1962, p. 6), its curriculum centered on the Bible and religious practice. All other studies supported and confirmed this ardent Puritan orthodoxy which had been inherited from the Calvinist Reformed university teaching and traditions. This imbued arts education thus represented "godly learning," for it "never escaped its purposeful role in the pursuit of godliness" (Morgan, 1986, pp. 261–263). Tutors played the major role in students' development through daily instruction, the teaching of religious tenets, and the enforcing of discipline in study halls and dormitories (Finkelstein, 1983).

Later, Harvard graduates would also be the leading force for reform, as theology began to lose its influence to broader moral philosophy (Burton, 1996, pp. 11–12). Similarly, following the Cambridge residential model tailored to meet colonial needs, Harvard boarded students who were only in their early teens. Its residence halls became places for religious living rather than just intellectual development following the Oxbridge model (Cowley, 1934). Yet this goal also needed to be enforced. Student discipline problems pointed to the occurrence of debauchery, drunkenness, and rioting that was often met with fines, loss of privileges, or expulsions (Moore, 1976). Similar to colonial religious society, Harvard embraced all aspects of this theological worldview. Its collegiate ideal thus represented a Puritan center of higher learning where all things began and ended with the divine. Later, with the coming of the Great Awakening, conflicts over theological ideas and worship regulations shattered Harvard's godly Veritas (Bailyn, 1986), ultimately resulting in the creation of eight other colonial colleges where students were taught and lived according to similar, yet distinct, theological teachings. The colonial way thus comprised a New England religious community of learning and right behavior that was fused to a theological worldview whether students intended divine or secular occupations.

The Frontier Way. Victory over the British in the Revolution left these extensive former colonial lands in new hands. The process of state unification to form a new government proved to be a difficult task. Indeed, the Articles of Confederation were not strong enough to govern the existing or new states for very long. Only with the ratification of the Constitution in 1789 did a federal nation emerge. By 1800, the new republic numbered some 5.3 million inhabitants. Population streams extended settlement out from the coast to the frontiers of New York, Pennsylvania, the Ohio Valley, Kentucky, Tennessee, and western Georgia along roads and waterways. These movements enabled English, Welsh, Scotch-Irish, and German groups to begin farming and to create their own communities. One of their early concerns focused on providing education for their offspring (Meinig, 1986). Douglas Hurt in his book, *The Ohio Frontier: Crucible of the Old Northwest, 1720–1830* (1996), offers a valuable contextual overview of these advancements along the frontier. As family offspring could no longer find local farmland, they sought to educate themselves. Between 1800 and 1860, many poor young men entered local colleges (Allmendinger, 1975; Burke, 1982). During this antebellum era, log colleges and Mark Hopkinses gradually gave way to more permanent buildings and many faculty members as enrollments increased. Nevertheless, these schools were still products of the frontier.

Two major agencies, the states and religious denominations, sought to advance higher learning. Without federal government provision for such activity, support often came from the newly emerging states. Some dozen early state universities attempted to offer higher education, with the University of Virginia in 1824 and the University of Michigan in 1837 being the most influential examples (Brubacher and Rudy, 1997). At many other state institutions, Presbyterians, who became the most influential Christian denomination in higher education at this time, asserted controlling interests as trustees, presidents, and faculty leaders to such a great extent that state support and denominational designs merged, as may be seen at Ohio and Miami universities (Marsden, 1994; Rudolph, 1962).

Yet insufficient funding and political indifference left these few state-supported institutions in relatively weak positions to respond to the increasing local demands for higher education. As part of the development of town life everywhere (Potts, 1977), the task of establishing and funding colleges then fell most often to Christian denominations and churches. The "college movement" became an integral part of the "home missionary movement," as various religious groups sought to advance new evangelical designs on the frontier populations (Rudolph, 1962, pp. 52–53). For example, in Pennsylvania, of the thirty-one colleges founded before the Civil War, only sixteen continued after the war, and nine of those which continued were established by Presbyterians (Baltzell, 1996). In Ohio, twenty-three colleges were also begun during the same time period, twenty-one by religious groups, five of them by the Methodists (Geiger, 1995). In other states, such as Kentucky, Kansas, and Minnesota, "colleges were often founded right on the frontier line not a generation after the founding of a town" (Church and Sedlak, 1976, p. 140).

Recent interpretations of this college movement, as it reached mid-century, have characterized these and later institutions as "multilevel" and "multipurpose" entities (Burke, 1982; Leslie, 1992; Geiger 1995) offering collegiate, school, and trade programs. As older colonial colleges allowed students to board in town or on farms, frontier colleges permitted their students to do likewise. Self-reliance displaced institutional community (Allmendinger, 1975). These schools, particularly Oberlin, further enabled women and African Americans to attend (Fletcher, 1943; Hurt, 1996).

Before the Civil War, many schools opened their doors to all local students regardless of religious affiliation, if they would follow pan-Protestant liberal and enlightened ideals and practices. This was particularly true among New School Presbyterians who resisted sectarianism (Marsden, 1994). Such was the spirit of these frontier colleges where town boosterism, religious control, and local student desire provided the means to offer classical and practical education. Perhaps, Brubacher and Rudy said it best:

> In their social organization, the frontier denominational colleges seemed to bear out the truth of Frederick Jackson Turner's thesis about the transforming effects

of the American westward movement. They were more democratic in spirit than contemporary colleges in the East; they showed greater readiness to open doors to women on an equal footing with men; they snubbed snobbery and excluded exclusiveness. The multiplication of these colleges along a succession of frontiers undoubtedly furthered the broadening and democratization of American higher education, as well as its decentralization and diversification [1997, p. 73].

The development of scientific institutes, people's colleges, and land-grant colleges continued to differentiate these types of frontier institutions during the rest of the century (Johnson, 1981). Thus the American colonial college ideal went through radical transformations as the frontier way of life, self-reliance, denominational theology and morality, and broader educational offerings in the back country, as it was called (Meinig, 1986), characterized these new foundations and their spirit west of the Alleghenies. Its heritage may still best be seen in the religious-sponsored college of today (Pfnister, 1962).

The Collegiate Way. The development of cities, industries, and transportation systems as well as the expansion of agriculture after the Civil War brought great wealth to the North (Meinig, 1993). Now that unification of the nation was won, prestigious Yankee families funneled their monies into the colleges where they sent their children. "American education was entering a new epoch. Under the stimulus of increased endowments the leading colleges were enlarging their faculties, erecting new buildings, adding to their scientific equipment, broadening their curricula to include art, engineering, economics, and other neglected fields of study, bettering the methods of teaching, seeking to arouse the intellectual curiosity of their students" (Wertenbaker, 1946, p. 290).

Developments at Princeton seemed to exemplify the older institutions of higher learning in this new age. In 1868, as the newly installed University President, James McCosh created a new intellectual atmosphere on campus through the building of a recitation hall, library, science hall, three dormitories, a museum, and a chapel; through the hiring of ten additional professors; through allowing collegiate sports; and through the introduction of a more scientific curriculum (Wertenbaker, 1946). During the twenty years of his revitalization of the campus, the president raised some $3 million from new wealthy industrialists and increased the student body from 264 at the beginning of his presidency to 604 in 1888 at its end (Leslie, 1992).

As Rudolph described so well above, the collegiate way embodied a "residential scheme of things" in which students became a family and did all things together under one roof, as it were, under the guidance of the faculty. Students augmented their lives with co-and extra-curricular learning from literary societies, debating clubs, recreation and sports, as well as other less well-known pursuits. Generally campus residences remained in this era "places for students merely to sleep, to eat, and occasionally to study" (Cowley, 1934). It would not be until the latter part of the 20th century that their educational value would be enhanced and linked more directly to the curriculum. Meanwhile, New England presidents and their campuses, such as Smith of Dartmouth, Porter of Yale, and later Palmer of Wellesley, fostered—and came to represent—this new style of residential learning community (Rudolph, 1962).

Similarly, as the land changed from the frontier to established towns and cities across the new Middle West, surviving colleges also added student dormitories to their campuses. Older colleges sought to expand their enrollments by embracing coeducation, while new institutions, particularly those for women and African Americans, arose to provide other clienteles this type of collegiate residential education. According to Barbara Solomon, of 1,082 colleges in 1890, 43 percent were coeducational, 37 percent were for men only, and 20 percent were for women only (1985). Certainly, Mount Holyoke, Wellesley, Smith, and Vassar represented the women's collegiate way. Even though most turn-of-the-century American universities discouraged such residential plans, a new housing revival occurred across campuses when Yale, Chicago, Princeton, and later Harvard built residence halls to support undergraduate campus life (Cowley, 1934, pp. 759–761). The residential way thus became a mainstay of American collegiate life, often housed in dramatic Tudor Gothic buildings symbolizing the timeless heritage of liberal learning (Goodchild, 1998).

During this century, the residential way came to be synonymous with the liberal arts college, which initially faced a barrage of criticism. During the first decade, attacks on the college focused on its failure to identify its purpose, on its being too superficial, and on its irrelevancy to the contemporary world. Flexner (1908, pp. 3–11) further decried the "lack of intellectual stamina" of its graduates. Later, Kirkpatrick (1926) demanded greater student liberty in curricular choices, which would promote greater intellectual growth. This onslaught against (what was then called) the cultural college implored college leaders to introduce more electivism and research demands into its curricula, in other words, to impose the research university agenda on the American college. In response, Dartmouth President Ernest Martin Hopkins (1916) defended the use of philosophy, art, and literature as essential to the development of future leaders of character.

After World War I, greater clarity arose about the institution's purpose. Peyton Jacob (1931) of Mercer University noted in "The Enduring Function of the Changing College" that the four functions of the college were: (1) to offer broad general courses, (2) to introduce students to academic specialization, (3) to provide preprofessional training, and (4) to promote a civilizing function. In the mid–1930s, James Bryant Conant, president of Harvard, focused on the heart of the collegiate ideal issue when he spoke to the entering freshman students who faced a world challenged by Nazi aggression.

> To my mind, one of the most important aspects of a college education is that it provides a vigorous stimulus to independent thinking. The tremendous range of human knowledge covered by the curriculum, the diverse opinions expressed by the professors, the interminable arguments with your friends; all these contribute to feed the intellectual curiosity of all but the most complacent student. A desire to know more about the different sides of a question, a craving to

understand something of the opinions of other peoples and other times mark
the educated man. Education should not put the mind in a strait-jacket of conventional formulas but should provide it with the nourishment on which it may
unceasingly expand and grow. Think for yourselves! Absorb knowledge wherever possible and listen to the opinions of those more experienced than your-
self, but don't let any one do your thinking for you [1935, p. 449].

Conant understood the power of thinking, learning from faculty and peers,
and the means for this to occur. This liberal education thus encouraged a "disciplined mind" where knowledge, critical thinking, imagination, and moral values coalesced to produce a new intellectual outlook on life (Schmidt, 1962).
The residential way provided the means to achieve this new outlook.

After World War II, the federal government, through its National Defense
Education Act of 1958 and Higher Education Facilities Act of 1963, provided
monies for the construction of residence halls on university campuses to meet
escalating enrollments. This effort enabled administrators to develop the educational value of collegiate housing during the past 30 years (Frederiksen,
1993; Schroeder, Mable, and Associates, 1994). Without this federal enhancement, the residential way, especially among undergraduate students on university campuses (for example, the University College at Michigan State
University [Dressel, 1964] or the Cluster Colleges at the University of California, Santa Cruz [Grant and Riesman,1978]), would have remained marginally
effective in promoting their psychosocial development (Sanford, 1967).
Despite such support, the traditional residential public and private liberal arts
college has declined in numbers from 721 in 1970 to some 637 in 1994
(Carnegie Foundation, 1994; Keeton, 1971). Nevertheless, as Rudolph put it
so well (1962, p. 88), this collegiate pattern "had become a tradition, and from
then on the founders of American colleges either adhered to the tradition or
clumsily sought a new rationale."

The Town Way. Yet other ways and rationales were possible and, in fact,
needed. As New England, Middle Western, and Western colleges came into
being between 1870 and 1930, their founders built on the remaining lands,
either on the "hilltops" of the East (Brubacher and Rudy, 1997, p. 40), on the
fringes of midwestern town expansion (Reinert, 1970), or as part of the western city landscapes (Breck, 1989). They celebrated and enjoyed small town
and later large city closeness. In this developing collegiate ideal, it would
become the urban way for freestanding four-year colleges, university colleges
(that is, undergraduate colleges within universities where working students
attended part-time), and all undergraduate programs where living off, but near,
campus occurred.

In the 19th century, for poorer students who could not afford residential life or for campus leaders who eschewed dormitories, the town and
urban way became the choice of necessity. A glimpse of Amherst just after
the Civil War from the eyes of new student John W. Burgess, the future Roo-
sevelt professor and dean of political science at Columbia University, pro-

vides a deeper understanding of the town way. In the fall of 1864, after having fought in the war, Burgess arrived at Amherst and was taken by a friend to the top of its College Chapel's tower to see the campus, town, and surrounding countryside.

> Down to that moment of my life, I had never seen anything quite so beautiful in scenery as the view from that spot. The chapel and the college buildings generally were situated upon a hill rising out of the east side of the Connecticut valley, having the Holyoke range for its boundary on the south, Mt. Toby and Mt. Sugar Loaf on the north, the Pelham hills on the east and, in the far distance on the west, the blue hills of Berkshire, with the winding Connecticut in the middle ground. The foliage was just putting on those vivid and varied hues for which middle New England scenery in autumn is so justly noted and admired. And overall was spread such an air of peace, contentment, and good will as made the earth to me a different place to live in from what I had elsewhere found it [Burgess, 1934, p. 38].

Burgess had viewed the arcadia of inspiration and contemplation, the renowned nineteenth century New England summer experience where college professors often wrote their greatest works. Yet where would Burgess live? Facing the town common was a boarding house, operated by two landladies. He joined his friend's fraternity, whose members lived on one of the boarding house floors, to acquire this lodging, where the women maintained order and provided the food (Burgess, 1934). The town provided basic necessities, while the college expanded the mind. Again representing the best romantic hagiography of yesterday, Burgess spoke to this point in finding Professor Julius H. Seelye among the faculty:

> After the first hour with him, I had the very strong and decided feeling that he was the man for whom I had been all my previous life looking. . . . His was the keenest, largest intellect of the faculty, and his acquirements were prodigious. He was theologian, natural scientist, historian, lawyer, litterateur, everything, and he attacked the problems of philosophy from every point of view.
>
> His method of teaching was quite Socratic. He did not give set lectures, but he put a textbook, Hickok's Mental Science, Hickok's Moral Science, or Schwegler's History of Philosophy into the hands of his students and designated a certain lesson for each day. The lesson, however, was not a recitation, but a discussion between each and every member of the class and the professor in which the purpose was to develop the power of thinking, reasoning, and stating grounds on the part of each student. The exercises of his classroom were the most powerful incentive to thought and study I ever experienced in my entire life of study [1934, pp. 52–53].

Burgess's student days at Amherst later became faculty days as well. In the end, President Nicholas Murray Butler of Columbia offered both foreword and concluding remarks on Burgess's contributions to the university and American higher education for his autobiography.

Undoubtedly, Burgess's experience was not shared by all. Extensive analysis of Amherst in its earlier days showed the difficulties students, faculty, and townspeople faced with undisciplined students free from campus rules (Allmendinger, 1975). Yet Amherst, with its dedication to off-campus living in the 1800s, continued to demonstrate superior efforts in teaching and forming young minds, earning favorable attention from early and mid–twentieth century commentators (Brubacher and Rudy, 1997; Jencks and Riesman, 1968; Kirkpatrick, 1926; Rudolph, 1962).

Moreover, the expansion of higher education enrollments during the era presented campus presidents with a dilemma. Although enrollments swelled, these students were not living on campus. In fact, Amherst even shut down a new residence hall, because students preferred to live off campus. Concomitantly, the German university ideal persuaded many American university presidents not to build student residences. Further, many state universities at that time could not afford to build residence halls nor could their students afford their expense. As Cowley noted, these influences converged to produce a national transformation where the percentage of students living on campus declined from 53 percent in 1870 to only 24 percent in 1905 (1934, pp. 711–712). Thus, as this Amherst vignette demonstrates, powerful learning environments were created without corresponding campus residence experiences.

The Community Way. At the turn of this century, the growth of the American population due to immigration brought about extensive urbanization (Freeman and others, 1992). As youths of emerging racial, ethnic, and religious groups sought higher education, they were generally required to remain in their local communities, often working to afford postsecondary education. Students thus lived at home, which precluded them from attending traditional residential colleges. The new community way of obtaining higher learning while still residing with one's parents overcame this problem. In 1901, students enrolled at the first public junior college, Joliet Junior College, in Illinois. The junior college movement, as Cowley observed (1934, p. 712), reduced the need for residence halls, "because of the inability of many parents to educate their children away from home." By 1918, 85 junior colleges existed, educating 4,500 students. By the end of World War II, the number of two-year institutions had grown to 456. They provided general education for some 150,000 students; one of the most dramatic institutional developments, particularly for "practical-oriented, lower-middle-class students," in American higher education (Levine, 1986, p. 162). So successful were these institutions that the famous Truman Report on Higher Education (President's Commission on Higher Education, 1947) called on the federal and state governments to support these "community" colleges. During the next fifty-year transformation, these colleges began to shift from their single focus on general education, which could be transferred to four-year institutions, to include also vocational education (Brint and Karabel, 1989).

In 1995, some 1,500 community colleges provided adults extensive opportunities to further their learning and education. Other institutions, often called "street-car colleges," arose during this century to accommodate youths and adults who wanted post-secondary education in urban areas (Riesman and Jencks, 1967, pp. 105–107). The rise of extension education, summer schools, and proprietary education resulted from progressivist impulses in the early part of the century (Cremin, 1988). Later, increasing demand for higher education brought the establishment of nontraditional schools: University Without Walls colleges (for example, Antioch College, Goddard College, Morgan State College, and others [Houle, 1973]); competence-based colleges (for example, Alverno College and the School for New Learning at DePaul University [Apps, 1988]); multi-disciplinary colleges (for example, Evergreen State College, Hampshire College [Grant and Riesman, 1978], and the General College at the University of Minnesota [Cremin, 1988]); and self-paced individualized programs (for example, Empire State College and Minnesota Metropolitan University [Grant and Riesman, 1978]). Thus almost anyone could obtain a college education, while remaining at home. In 1988, Apps called on faculty to confront the challenges of this new, transformed "learning society," where reaching part-time older students, understanding their learning needs, and using community resources to assist their learning represented the critical need of contemporary higher education (p. 200).

The Distance Way. Now in the 1990s, advances in technology enable distance education to be the way of the future. Students no longer need to leave home to obtain a college education; faculty can deliver learning via the Internet and email to the house or office. The history of distance education can be traced to correspondence courses, then statewide audiobridge classes, and finally the use of video through satellite transmissions throughout the nation (Dunning, Van Kekerix, and Zaborowski, 1993; Kett, 1994). In August 1985, National Technological University provided some 80 courses by satellite to corporate clients across the United States. Its campus became the boardroom. Similarly, the Electronic University Network enabled campuses to deliver their courses via home computers to associate and baccalaureate students of Thomas A. Edison State College and to master's in business administration students of John F. Kennedy University (Apps, 1988). During the early 1990s, Mind Extension University at Jones Intercable enabled the University of Maryland and Regis University to offer baccalaureate degrees nationally through cable television (Goodchild, 1997). By this time, many states, including Iowa, Oklahoma, Texas, Wisconsin, and Wyoming, had created statewide two-way audio and video networks to link campuses with learners, which required greater statewide higher education coordination and planning (Epper, 1997).

Through the efforts of the Western Interstate Commission for Higher Education, sixteen western states in conjunction with public and private institutions of higher learning began offering distance courses through Western Governors University in late 1998. One of the more recent efforts spans the globe. In 1994, the Colorado Electronic Community College began offering an associates degree from the eleven-member community college system by way of the Internet; some 200 students from as far away as Russia have taken courses and completed degrees (Susman, 1998). Because of distance education, the classroom has been transformed to become simultaneously residential and global. Its challenge is to create a cyberspace community of learning where students can develop intellectually, socially, and morally.

Conclusion

These six historic ways of learning provide a framework to understand the evolving American collegiate ideal. Each has offered a place for higher learning, whether it has been through a colonial, frontier, collegiate, town, community, or distance way. Each has created a community of learners where students have embraced, partially or fully, a new intellectual spirit which has changed their lives (Meiklejohn, 1920). Such communities have often availed themselves of faculty mentors (Boyer, 1987), peer groups (Newcombe, 1967; Astin, 1993), or co-curricular and service learning (Jacoby, 1996; Kuh, Schuh, Whitt, and Associates, 1991) to achieve higher learning. Yet a more comprehensive vision of the collegiate purpose and ideal for the twenty-first century is still lacking. Its creation undoubtedly will be dependent upon the more recent insights from another significant higher education scholar who explored the purposeful, open, just, disciplined, caring, and celebratory attributes of campus community. Ernest Boyer's last major work on this issue, *Campus Life: In Search of Community,* points to a future seventh way which epitomizes the collegiate ideal of these six predecessors.

> What is needed, we believe, is a larger, more integrative vision of community in higher education, one that focuses not only on the length of time students spend on campus, but on the quality of the encounter, and relates not only to social activities, but to the classroom, too. The goal as we see it is to clarify both academic and civic standards, and above all, to define with some precision the enduring values that undergird a community of learning. In the end, building a vital community is a challenge confronting not just higher learning, but the whole society. In our hard-edged competitive world, more humane, more integrative purposes must be defined. And perhaps it is not too much to hope that as colleges and universities affirm a new vision of community on campus, they may also promote the common good in the neighborhood, the nation, and the world [Carnegie Foundation for the Advancement of Teaching, 1990, pp. 7, 67].

References

Allmendinger, Jr., D. F. *Paupers and Scholars: The Transformation of Student Life in Nineteenth-Century New England.* New York: St. Martin's Press, 1975.

Apps, J. W. *Higher Education in a Learning Society: Meeting New Demands for Education and Training.* San Francisco: Jossey-Bass, 1988.

Astin, A. W. *What Matters in College? Four Critical Years Revisited.* San Francisco: Jossey-Bass, 1993.

Bailyn, B. "Foundations." In Bailyn, B., Fleming, D., Handlin, O., and Thernstrom, S, *Glimpses of the Harvard Past.* Cambridge, Mass.: Harvard University Press, 1986.

Baltzell, E. D. *Puritan Boston and Quaker Philadelphia.* New Brunswick, N.J.: Transaction Publishers, 1996. (Originally published 1979.)

Boorstin, D. J. *The Americans: The National Experience.* New York: Vintage Books, 1965.

Boyer, E. L. *College: The Undergraduate Experience in America.* Carnegie Foundation for the Advancement of Teaching. New York: Harper and Row, 1987.

Breck, A. D. *From the Rockies to the World: A Companion to the History of the University of Denver, 1864–1989.* Denver, Colo.: Hirschfeld Press, 1989.

Brint, S., and Karabel, J. *The Diverted Dream: Community Colleges and the Promise of Educational Opportunity in America, 1900–1985.* New York: Oxford University Press, 1989.

Brubacher, J. S., and Rudy, W. *Higher Education in Transition: A History of American Colleges and Universities.* (4th ed.) New Brunswick, N.J.: Transaction Publishers, 1997.

Burgess, J. W. *Reminiscences of an American Scholar: The Beginnings of Columbia University.* Foreword by N. M. Butler. Morningside Heights, N.Y.: Columbia University Press, 1934.

Burke, C. B. *American Collegiate Populations: A Test of the Traditional View.* New York: New York University Press, 1982.

Burton, J. D. "The Harvard Tutors: The Beginnings of an Academic Profession." *History of Higher Education Annual,* 1996, *16,* 5–20.

Carnegie Foundation for the Advancement of Teaching. *Campus Life: In Search of Community.* Foreword by E. L. Boyer. New York: Harper and Row, 1990.

Carnegie Foundation for the Advancement of Teaching. *A Classification of Institutions of Higher Education, 1994 Edition.* Foreword by E. L. Boyer. Princeton, N.J., 1994.

Church, R. L., and Sedlak, M. W. *Education in the United States: An Interpretive History.* New York: Free Press, 1976.

Clark, B. R. *The Distinctive College: Antioch, Reed, and Swarthmore.* Chicago: Aldine, 1970.

Conant, J. B. "Address to Freshmen in Harvard College." *School and Society,* 1935, *42* (1084), 449–451.

Cowley, W. H. "The History of Student Residential Housing, II." *School and Society,* 1934, *40* (1040), 705–712, 758–764.

Cremin, L. A. *American Education: The Metropolitan Experience, 1876–1980.* New York: Harper and Row, 1988.

Cremin, L. A. *The Transformation of the School: Progressivism in American Education, 1876–1957.* New York: Vintage Books, 1961.

Dressel, P. L. "Educational Innovations at Michigan State University." In W. H. Stickler (ed.), *Experimental Colleges: Their Role in American Higher Education.* Tallahassee, Fla.: Florida State University, 1964.

Elazar, D. J. *American Federalism: A View from the States.* New York: Thomas Y. Crowell, 1966.

Elazar, D. J. *Cities of the Prairie: The Metropolitan Frontier and American Politics.* New York: Basic Books, 1970.

Epper, R. M. "Coordination and Competition in Postsecondary Distance Education: A Comparative Case Study of Statewide Policies." *Journal of Higher Education,* 1997, *68* (5), 551–587.

Finkelstein, M. "From Tutor to Specialized Scholar: Academic Professionalization in Eighteenth and Nineteenth Century America." *History of Higher Education Annual,* 1983, *3,* 99–121.

Fletcher, R. S. *A History of Oberlin College: From Its Foundation Through the Civil War.* 2 vols. Oberlin, Ohio: Oberlin College, 1943.

Flexner, A. *The American College: A Criticism.* New York: Century, 1908.

Frederiksen, C. F. "A Brief History of Collegiate Housing." In R. B. Winston, Jr., S. Anchors, and Associates (eds.). *Student Housing and Residential Life: A Handbook for Professionals Committed to Student Development Goals.* Foreword by H. C. Riker. San Francisco: Jossey-Bass, 1993.

Freeman, J., and others. *Who Built America? Working People and the Nation's Economy, Politics, Culture, and Society,* Vol. 2: *From the Gilded Age to the Present.* American Social History Project. New York: Pantheon Books, 1992.

Geiger, R. L. "The Era of Multipurpose Colleges in American Higher Education, 1850–1890." *History of Higher Education Annual*, 1995, *15*, 51–92.

Goodchild, L. F. "Contemporary Undergraduate Education: An Era of Alternatives and Reassessment." *Theory Into Practice*, 1997, *36* (2), 123–131.

Goodchild, L. F. "The Mission of the Catholic University in the Midwest, 1842–1980: A Comparative Case Study of the Effects of Strategic Policy Decisions Upon the Mission of the University of Notre Dame, Loyola University of Chicago, and DePaul University." Unpublished doctoral dissertation, University of Chicago, 1986.

Goodchild, L. F. "Oxbridge's Tudor Gothic Influences on American Academic Architecture." Paper presented at the 20th annual meeting of the International Standing Conference for the History of Education, Belgium, 1998.

Grant, G., and Riesman, D. *The Perpetual Dream: Reform and Experiment in the American College*. Chicago: University of Chicago Press, 1978.

Hopkins, E. M. "The College of the Future." *School and Society*, 1916, *4* (95), 609–617.

Houle, C. O. *The External Degree*. Foreword by S. B. Gould. San Francisco: Jossey-Bass, 1973.

Hurt, R. D. *The Ohio Frontier: Crucible of the Old Northwest, 1720–1830. A History of the Trans-Appalachian Frontier*. Bloomington, Ind.: Indiana University Press, 1996.

Jacob, P. "The Enduring Function of the Changing College." *Peabody Journal of Education*, 1931, *9* (3), 131–142.

Jacoby, B. *Service-Learning in Higher Education: Concepts and Practices*. Foreword by T. Ehrlich. San Francisco: Jossey-Bass, 1996.

Jencks, C., and Riesman, D. *The Academic Revolution*. New York: Doubleday, 1968.

Johnson, E. L. "Misconceptions About the Early Land-Grant Colleges." *Journal of Higher Education*, 1981, *53* (4), 333–351.

Keeton, M. T. *Models and Mavericks: A Profile of Private Liberal Arts Colleges*. Carnegie Commission on Higher Education. New York: McGraw-Hill, 1971.

Kett, J. F. *The Pursuit of Knowledge Under Difficulties: From Self-Improvement to Adult Education in America, 1750–1990*. Stanford, Calif.: Stanford University Press, 1994.

Kirkpatrick, J. E. *The American College and Its Rulers*. New York: New Republic, 1926.

Kuh, G. D., Schuh, J. H., Whitt, E. J., and Associates. *Involving Colleges: Successful Approaches to Fostering Student Learning and Development Outside the Classroom*. San Francisco: Jossey-Bass, 1991.

Lawlis, C. L. *Vincennes University in Transition: The Making of a Comprehensive Community College*. Vincennes, Ind.: Vincennes University, 1982.

Leslie, W. B. *Gentlemen and Scholars: College and Community in the "Age of the University," 1865–1917*. University Park, Pa.: Pennsylvania State University Press, 1992.

Levine, D. O. *The American College and the Culture of Aspiration, 1915–1940*. Ithaca, N.Y.: Cornell University Press, 1986.

Marsden, G. M. *The Soul of the American University: From Protestant Establishment to Established Nonbelief*. New York: Oxford University Press, 1994.

Martin, W. B. *The College of Character: Renewing the Purpose and Content of College Education*. Jossey-Bass Series in Higher Education. San Francisco: Jossey-Bass, 1982.

Meiklejohn, A. *The Experimental College*. New York: Harper and Brothers, 1932.

Meiklejohn, A. *The Liberal College. American Education: Its Men, Ideas and Institutions*. New York: Arno Press, 1969. (Originally published 1920.)

Meinig, D. W. *The Shaping of America: A Geographical Perspective on 500 Years of History*, Vol. 1: *Atlantic America, 1492–1800*. Vol. 2: *Continental America, 1800–1867*. New Haven, Conn.: Yale University Press, 1986, 1993.

Miller, P. *The New England Mind: The Seventeenth Century*. Cambridge, Mass.: Harvard University Press, 1939.

Moore, K. M. "Freedom and Constraint in Eighteenth Century Harvard." *Journal of Higher Education*, 1976, *47* (6), 649–659.

Morgan, J. *Godly Learning: Puritan Attitudes towards Reason, Learning and Education, 1560–1640*. Cambridge: Cambridge University Press, 1986.

Morison, S. E. *The Founding of Harvard College.* Cambridge, Mass.: Harvard University Press, 1935.

Newcombe, T. M. "Student Peer-Group Influence." In N. Sanford (ed.), *The American College: A Psychological and Social Interpretation of Higher Learning.* New York: Wiley, 1967.

Pfnister, A. O. "A Century of the Church-Related College." In W. W. Brickman and S. Lehrer (eds.), *A Century of Higher Education: Classical Citadel to Collegiate Colossus.* New York: Society for the Advancement of Education, 1962.

Potts, D. B. "'College Enthusiasm!' As Public Response, 1800–1860." *Harvard Educational Review,* 1977, 47 (1), 28–42.

President's Commission on Higher Education. *Higher Education for American Democracy.* New York: Harper, 1947

Reinert, SJ, P. C. *The Urban Catholic University.* New York: Sheed and Ward, 1970.

Riesman, D., and Jencks, C. "The Viability of the American College." In N. Sanford (ed.), *The American College: A Psychological and Social Interpretation of Higher Learning.* New York: Wiley, 1967.

Rohrbough, M. J. *The Land Office Business: The Settlement and Administration of American Public Lands, 1789–1837.* New York: Oxford University Press, 1968.

Rudolph, F. *The American College and University: A History.* New York: Vintage Press, 1962.

Sanford, N. (ed.). *The American College: A Psychological and Social Interpretation of Higher Learning.* New York: Wiley, 1967.

Schmidt, G. P. "A Century of the Liberal Arts College." In W. W. Brickman and S. Lehrer (eds.), *A Century of Higher Education: Classical Citadel to Collegiate Colossus.* New York: Society for the Advancement of Education, 1962.

Schroeder, C. C., Mable, P., and Associates. *Realizing the Educational Potential of Residence Halls.* Foreword by T. J. Marchese. San Francisco: Jossey-Bass, 1994.

Solomon, B. M. *In the Company of Educated Women: A History of Women and Higher Education in America.* New Haven, Conn.: Yale University Press, 1985.

Staloff, D. *The Making of an American Thinking Class: Intellectuals and Intelligentsia in Puritan Massachusetts.* New York: Oxford University Press, 1998.

Susman, M. B. "Colorado Electronic Community College / Arapahoe Community College." [http://www.meu.edu/cc/univs/cecc.html]. 1998.

Wade, R. C. *The Urban Frontier: Pioneer Life in Early Pittsburgh, Cincinnati, Lexington, Louisville, and St. Louis.* Cambridge, Mass.: Harvard University Press, 1959.

Wertenbaker, T. J. *Princeton, 1746–1896.* Princeton, N.J.: Princeton University Press, 1946.

LESTER F. GOODCHILD *is professor of higher education at the University of Denver.*

While often considered an elitist concept, the collegiate ideal has changed over time to become a more pluralistic model with benefits for diverse students.

The Diverse Campus: Broadening Our Ideal to Incorporate All Voices

Adrianna J. Kezar

Until higher education expanded into more accessible forms with broader enrollments, such as community colleges and comprehensive institutions, the collegiate "ideal" was traditionally associated with the elite education received by eighteen- to twenty-two-year-old white men (Levine and Cureton, 1998). Because this expensive and exclusive education is associated with this group of students and with an elite environment, the collegiate ideal is often looked upon as antithetical to efforts to diversify post-secondary institutions. The assumption, however, that the collegiate ideal is antithetical to a diverse environment is inaccurate and presents a distorted picture of the potential of the collegiate ideal for facilitating learning among diverse students. The purpose of this chapter is to uncouple the concept of the collegiate environment from this elitist, exclusive image and to illustrate how the assumptions of this environment *are* compatible with a pluralistic campus.

I present four sets of evidence illustrating that the collegiate environment can be (and has become) aligned with the concept of a pluralistic learning environment. First, I describe how the collegiate environment has been associated with positive impacts for some non-traditional students, looking primarily at women and students of color. Second, I present evidence that the traditional aspects of a collegiate environment have changed over time to incorporate diverse students' styles, preferences, and experiences. Third, I suggest how changes in technology and the de-emphasis on location can have negative consequences for women, students of color, and other non-traditional students. Fourth, I note how diversity and pluralism strengthen the collegiate ideal. What is clear is that institutions should exercise great care in considering a move away from the collegiate ideal. When incorporating new approaches to post-secondary education, we must keep the benefits of the collegiate way for all students in the forefront of these discussions. In short, a pluralistic environment can complement the collegiate ideal just as the collegiate ideal can complement enhancing pluralism on campus.

Collegiate Environment: Positive Outcomes for Diverse Students

A key pattern in the research on collegiate environmental factors is that there is no significant difference between students of color and Caucasians in terms of the positive benefits of the collegiate environment. Close relationships with faculty, peer group influence, out-of-classroom experiences, and living on campus are all associated with increased student learning outcomes, persistence, educational attainment (obtaining one's desired educational objective), and satisfaction with the college experience. Research by Kuh, Astin, Pascarella and Terenzini, Feldman and Newcomb, and the National Center for Post-Secondary Teaching, Learning, and Assessment all illustrate the contributions of out-of-classroom experiences (Bean and Metzner, 1996; Kuh and others, 1994; Terenzini, 1993). These out-of-classroom experiences (involvement with peer groups, campus-based groups, student government, residence halls) are the same qualities associated with the collegiate environment.

Three theories underlie the positive impact of these factors: the involvement principle, person-environment interaction frameworks, and the close relationship between learning and personal development. The involvement principle posits that "the more time and energy students spend on purposeful activities, the more they benefit" (Kuh and others, 1994, p. 12). The amount of educational benefit is directly related to the quality and quantity of a student's investment of time and energy. Person–environment theories suggest that the environment has a significant impact on learning. Those who have studied learning from a sociological perspective provide evidence that the classroom is a narrow perspective for measuring learning outcomes. Lastly, several scholars have posited that the domains of learning and personal development are inextricably linked (Kuh and others, 1994). Thus, it is the opportunities for involvement, out-of-classroom experiences, and other characteristics of the collegiate environment that have a significant positive impact on students in a variety of ways.

In addition to the generalized research about the positive impact of collegiate environments for all students, several studies suggest that the principles underlying the collegiate environment are extremely important for certain groups of nontraditional students and increase their success (Ratcliff and others, 1996). It has also been found that nonresidential college students of color find the transition to college to be more difficult (Terenzini and others, 1996; Smith, 1993). Living on campus or being part of a learning community facilitates several factors that are important to student success, including validating experiences—defined as experiences that are empowering, confirming, and supportive (Schein and Bowers, 1992; Smith, 1993). Finding someone who cares coupled with out-of-classroom experiences is critical to success among first generation college students (Terenzini and others, 1996).

Uri Triesman developed successful communities for minority college students who were unsuccessful in calculus classes even though they had the academic prerequisites. He determined that diverse learners could thrive by creating a personalized and community-oriented environment that took students' backgrounds and characteristics into account (Kuh and others, 1994). Examples of the success of residential environments for minority and first-generation college students include the twenty-first century and the WISE programs at the University of Michigan; similar programs exist across the country (Kanoy, Bruhn, and Woodson, 1996; Stinson, 1990). These programs house first generation college students or women studying math, science, and engineering together so that they can develop a sense of community and support. These students enroll in similar courses and are involved in out-of-classroom activities together. Thus, the characteristics of a collegiate environment are associated with positive learning outcomes for minority and first generation students.

Another factor leading to success among first-generation college students is having someone who cares about their success (Terenzini and others, 1996). Caring could be found through a connectedness and a sense of belonging often associated with interaction with others on campus and with residential environments. A close relationship between faculty and students increases the likelihood of students finding someone who cares.

Peer groups have been shown to have a profound impact on student learning (Astin, 1993; Feldman and Newcomb, 1969; Schroeder and Mable, 1996). The living and learning environments described above take advantage of the impact of residential settings on student learning and purposely structure environments to take advantage of cooperative learning and encourage students to learn from each other. On-campus living and residential peer influence have been shown to have significant influence on the success of African-American students as defined by GPA and retention (Nettles, Thoeney, and Gosman, 1996).

In studies on student satisfaction which look at racial, ethnic or gender based differences in students' perceptions of the collegiate ideal, the general pattern found is that students in all "minority" groups tend to find the same aspects of campuses positive. The institutional aspects that diverse students find positive include high levels of faculty-student interaction, living on campus, a student-centered environment, more resources spent on student affairs, and involvement indicators (Hurtado, Kezar, and Carter, 1995).

As is reinforced throughout this issue, involvement increases student learning (Astin, 1985). Research has found that many of the typical out-of-classroom experiences such as involvement with student government, athletics, and fraternities or sororities do have a positive impact on sense of belonging for students of color, yet involvement patterns differ. Hispanic students, for example, tend to be more involved with religious, community, and social organizations.

However, a corollary concern is that these out-of-classroom programs attempt to assimilate students into environments (Hurtado and Carter, 1996). Assimilation can result in cultural conflict, resistance, self-doubt, and other negatives outcomes. Thus, it is important to look at the ways that the college environment has changed to encompass more diverse students.

Broadening of the Collegiate Environment

Some scholars have suggested that many of the structures and cultural aspects of collegiate institutions are associated with a particularized way of organizing and reinforcing unequal power relationships, such as learning through competition, discrete, linear ways of knowing, and knowing separated from the object of study (Belenky, Clinchy, Goldberger, and Tarule, 1986). Several traditions have questioned whether this is the best learning environment for all learners. Feminist theory emphasizes that women learn better in relational and connected ways. In addition, African tradition (as well as other nonwestern traditions) has limited emphasis on the individual and stresses collectivity, affiliation, and interdependence (Cheatham, 1996). As a result, new forms of organizing learning have been developed that expand the ways that the collegiate learning environment is defined and experienced. Due to space constraints, I will describe only three of the major changes: (1) collaborative learning approaches; (2) learning communities; and, (3) community service learning. These new approaches to pedagogy and organizing the learning environment are responsive to concerns of equality, access, and creating an environment more desirable to diverse groups of students. All of these new pedagogical approaches reinforce the collegiate ideal.

Collaborative learning approaches have been promoted as an alternative to conventional forms of community in the classroom, which have been based on expertise, distance between faculty and students, and individual performance and assessment. Instead, collaborative learning emphasizes the importance of shared inquiry among students and faculty members. Feminist pedagogy and social constructivist theory posit that learners are diverse individuals whose understanding of reality is shaped by gender, race, class, age, and cultural experience (Maylath, 1991). Through this lens, learning, conceived as transmission of knowledge from the expert to the individual receiving learner, is inadequate. Instead, "to enable learners to move beyond superficial or merely procedural understanding of a subject, the teacher must invite them into a process of working out their own understandings and syntheses of the materials and developing their individual points of view toward it" (Belenky, Clinchy, Goldberger, and Tarule, 1986). Collaborative forms of learning break down the power distinctions between teacher and student. Teachers are active co-learners, and they attempt to share their expertise without eclipsing the students' beginning attempts to develop their own ideas. Studies of learning have illustrated that women and people of color prefer collaborative learning environments and have stronger learning outcomes when they are used (Berry, 1991; Rau and Heyl, 1990). Collaborative learning is also particularly important for adult learners who tend to feel more supported in environments that respect the knowledge they bring from outside the classroom (Bruffee, 1993).

Learning communities are curricular restructuring approaches that link or cluster classes around an interdisciplinary theme and enroll a common cohort of students. Learning communities are based on principles of collaborative learning and emphasize teamwork and common learning experiences (Levine and Tompkins, 1996). They also emphasize three newer concepts that assist in creating a more pluralistic environment for diverse types of students: (1) relational knowing; (2) trust; and (3) diverse forms of knowing. Studies illustrate that women tend to see connections between bodies of knowledge and see information as relational (Belenky, Clinchy, Goldberger, and Tarule, 1986; Geltner, 1994). Interdisciplinary approaches emphasize the relationships among various disciplines. In addition, learning communities emphasize knowledge as relational between people (not just between concepts). Again, studies illustrate that previously under-represented groups will feel more empowered in a familiar environment where they feel safe. Learning communities enroll students in common sets of courses permitting them to develop the types of relationships necessary to create a safe environment so that they can challenge the instructor and each other, talk in class, and question their beliefs. An additional benefit in moving toward a pluralistic environment is that more diverse perspectives tend to be brought up in the classroom (Smith, 1991). In an environment of trust and relationship, controversy and difference are more likely to emerge.

Learning communities are also successful within community colleges and large comprehensive or research universities where the collegiate ideal has never really existed. Learning communities allow for the goals of the collegiate ideal to be met within these large, often impersonal environments, where it is difficult to foster community (Tinto and Goodsell, 1995; Tinto and Russo, 1994).

Community service learning (CSL) is another pedagogical technique for broadening the collegiate ideal and has been associated with positive outcomes for women and minorities (Battistoni, 1995; Jacoby, 1996). Through CSL, students engage in community service as part of a class or activity and reflect on the service in relation to a course or a particular theme. Studies have illustrated that students who might not otherwise be engaged with the campus community find engagement through service (Batchelder and Root, 1994). There may be several reasons for CSL having such a positive impact on women, minorities and other disempowered groups. First, service has long been the domain of women. Second, many cultural groups, such as African-Americans, have strong service traditions tied to religion or community. Certainly community service has a long tradition within many liberal arts colleges in this country. But newer approaches to service learning emphasize that both the student and the community have equal power and learn from each other in the service learning process, as opposed to earlier forms of service where the volunteer was seen as possessing expertise and helping the disempowered community. Many argue the benefits of

CSL for all students because of its power to ground abstract knowledge in experience (Gorman and others, 1994; Luce and others, 1990; Warren and others, 1995). I am emphasizing the ways that this form of learning has transformed the learning environment for nontraditional students through an approach that is more aligned with a nonelitist form of collegiate learning.

Although the benefits of CSL have not been studied for adults, the benefits of other experiential forms of learning for adult learners have been documented by many studies (Warren and others, 1995). The National Society for Experiential Education (NSEE)—developed in the 1970s as more adult students were entering higher education—supports efforts to integrate experiential forms of learning into the post-secondary experience. This organization has helped campuses to develop internship, apprenticeship, study abroad, and community service learning programs. NSEE goals are building relationships for learning, communal and community-based learning, person-to-person contact in the learning environment, learning from each other, and expanding the place and time where learning occurs. These principles, which underlie the new pedagogical movements to incorporate diverse and individual students, are the same principles incorporated into the collegiate ideal.

The Move Away from the Collegiate Ideal

The adoption of technology to provide greater access to higher education has raised concern among some scholars and practitioners. Feminist scholars have voiced concern that teaching cannot be reduced to content and transmitting knowledge (as described in the section on collaborative learning). It is noted that the "body" and real physical contact are necessary for the process of teaching and learning in a constructivist epistemology (Irvine, 1998). Learning is associated not only with verbal, but also with nonverbal communication. Eye contact, physical gestures, and emotional cues are part of learning. Learning is also dependent on the energy created by students and faculty interacting (Shultz, 1988; Stanton and others, 1995).

Studies on the use of technology in the classroom have indicated that e-mail discussion groups are often less successful than in-class discussion groups. It is difficult to identify why this is true, but it is hypothesized that the inability to see nonverbal communication cues during e-mail discussions has a negative impact on the discussions and the resultant learning, while the interpersonal relationships developed in the classroom contribute positively to the learning process (Hall and Hall, 1991). Studies in distance learning tend to focus on content outcomes; almost no studies have explored broader sets of outcomes such as development, cognitive complexity, and humanitarianism (Stanton and others, 1995). Thus, it is difficult to identify whether they would or would not be able to enhance these other learning goals. Clearly this is an area in need of further research. It is hypothesized that technology is best used as a supplement to, not as a substitute for, in-class learning (O'Donnell, 1998).

There are also cultural differences in terms of verbal versus nonverbal communication and learning. African-American culture depends heavily on nonverbal communication (McGregory, 1989). Studies in science have also found that nonverbal communication is important for teaching in laboratory and group problem solving settings. Nonverbal communication is difficult to mimic through computer simulations (Priestley and others, 1997). There needs to be more research on the way learning is affected when in-person methods are not utilized and nonverbal communication is lost. The proposed research should examine differences among cultural groups as well as among individuals.

Others argue that technology can be used to reduce prejudice and culturally insensitive practices in which many faculty members unintentionally engage, although minimal research has been conducted in this area. The learning lost by subtracting the teacher does not justify nonhuman approaches that might temporarily protect students from a hostile learning environment. I believe we should continue to transform the collegiate environment rather than abandon it in efforts to create a less discriminatory environment. Technology may be an effective teaching mechanism for certain learning outcomes and among certain types of students. However, until there is research about the impact of moving away from traditional learning approaches to computer pedagogical approaches, it seems problematic to move away from the collegiate ideal.

Pluralism Enhancing the Collegiate Ideal

Much of the student affairs and learning literature emphasizes how attention to diverse students and recognizing and respecting differences help to enhance certain students' learning. More recent research emphasizes how a diverse environment is critical for learning and challenging stereotypes and preconceptions among all students (Cross, 1996). For example, Arthur Chickering and Linda Reisser argue that residence halls, learning communities, service experiences, and other collegiate structures and experiences are greatly enhanced when within a diverse climate (Astin, 1993; Chickering and Reisser, 1996; Kuh and others, 1994). Intergroup relations courses and learning communities have been developed on the notion (and research illustrates) that purposively placing a diverse group of students together in a supportive environment leads to outcomes such as cognitive complexity, understanding human differences, appreciation for the aesthetic qualities of life, and position-taking (Astin, 1993; Smith and others, 1994). Johnson, Johnson, and Smith posit that the process of "constructive controversy" underlies the growth and positive outcomes. Educational psychology research illustrates that conflict–difference can have many positive benefits including epistemic curiosity, reconceptualization of knowledge, and search for new knowledge if it is orchestrated positively in or out of the classroom (Johnson, Johnson, and Smith, 1996). Future research promises to show an even greater connection between diversity and enhanced learning outcomes that result from the struggle to develop community within a pluralistic environment. Results from studies of the impact of diversity on student learning (and initial results from longitudinal studies and ongoing research) clearly illustrate the importance of diversity and its connection with a whole array of learning outcomes (Smith and others, 1994).

Implications for Institutional Policy and Practice

Here are several recommendations for campuses. First, avoid the trap of believing the collegiate environment is automatically not beneficial to more diverse students. There is research that you can bring to the attention of colleagues who are suggesting dramatic changes to the campus that might take away the many benefits for students of color, women, or older students. This may seem contradictory to the findings in some of the chapters in this issue that suggest that we must alter our ideas about the collegiate ideal and resultant policy and practice. I am not suggesting that the collegiate ideal does not need to be modified. I am asking that we be careful and cautious, since principles undergirding this ideal have many advantages for all types of students. We should be striving for change rather than abandoning the ideal.

Second, attempt to obtain support for changes to existing structures and cultures on campus. Modifications to the current collegiate ideal can create environments more inclusive of a diverse student body. I have suggested the power of learning communities, collaborative learning, and community service learning as primary ways to modify the collegiate ideal.

Third, realize the dangers for many students in moving toward technology-based and distance education. I find it ironic that, as the student body becomes more diverse and women and minorities can benefit from education, there are financial pressures and arguments that institutions should move toward a type of education that appears less aligned with their learning styles. Furthermore, this form of pedagogy cannot, most likely, obtain the same goals as the collegiate ideal. The new group of diverse students should be able to reap the benefits of educating the whole student, which are obtained through relationships, community, out-of-classroom activities, and a sense of belonging or being cared for that are more easily fostered through the collegiate ideal. By decoupling the collegiate ideal from the traditional image of the student—and by becoming aware of the way the collegiate ideal can be (has been) altered to meet the needs of a more diverse student body—I hope you can see the promise of the collegiate ideal in the twenty-first century.

References

Astin, A. W. *Achieving Educational Excellence: A Critical Assessment of Priorities and Practices in Higher Education.* San Francisco: Jossey-Bass, 1985.

Astin A. W. *What Matters in College: Four Critical Years Revisited.* San Francisco: Jossey-Bass, 1993.

Batchelder, T., and Root, S. "Effects of an Undergraduate Program to Integrate Academic Learning and Service: Cognitive, Prosocial Cognitive, and Identity Outcomes." *Journal of Adolescence,* August 1994, 17 (4), 341–355.

Battistoni, R. "Service Learning, Diversity, and the Liberal Arts Curriculum." *Liberal Education,* 81 (1), 30–35, 1995.

Bean, J. P., and Metzner, B. S. "A Conceptual Model of Nontraditional Undergraduate Student Attrition." In F. K. Stage and others (eds.), *College Students: The Evolving Nature of Research.* Needham Heights, Mass.: Simon and Schuster, 1996, pp. 137–173.

Belenky, M., Clinchy, B., Goldberger, N., and Tarule, J. *Women's Ways of Knowing.* New York: Basic, 1986.

Berry, L., Jr. *Collaborative Learning: A Program for Improving the Retention of Minority Students,* 1991. (ED 384 323)

Bruffee, K. A. *Collaborative Learning: Higher Education, Interdependence, and the Authority of Knowledge,* 1993. (ED 364 160)

Cheatham, H. E. "Identity Development in a Pluralistic Society." In F. K. Stage and others (eds.), *College Students: The Evolving Nature of Research.* Needham Heights, Mass.: Simon and Schuster, 1996, pp. 205–216.

Chickering, A. W., and Reisser, L. "Key influences on Student Development." In F. K. Stage and others (eds.), *College Students: The Evolving Nature of Research.* Needham Heights, Mass.: Simon and Schuster, 1996, pp. 196–204.

Cross, P. K. "New Lenses on Learning." *About Campus,* 1996, *1* (1), 4–9.

Feldman, K. A., and Newcomb, T. *The Impact of College on Students.* San Francisco: Jossey-Bass, 1969.

Geltner, B. B. *The Power of Structural and Symbolic Redesign: Creating a Collaborative Learning Community in Higher Education.* Rochester, Mich.: Oakland University, 1994.

Gorman, M., and others. "Service Experience and the Moral Development of College Students." *Religious Education,* 1994, *89* (3), 422–431.

Hall, S., and Hall, P. *Between Schools: Inter-Classroom Collaboration,* 1991. (ED 333 481)

Hurtado, S., and Carter, D. F. "Latino Students' Sense of Belonging in the College Community: Rethinking the Concept of Integration on Campus." In F. K. Stage and others (eds.), *College Students: The Evolving Nature of Research.* Needham Heights, Mass.: Simon and Schuster, 1996, pp. 123–136.

Hurtado, S., Kezar, A., and Carter, D. "Understanding Student Satisfaction: An Exploration of Gender and Racial/Ethnic Differences Among College Students." Paper presented at the annual meeting of the American Education Research Association, San Francisco, Calif., April 15, 1995.

Irvine, L. "The Human Dimensions of Learning." Paper presented at the annual conference of the American Association of Colleges and Universities, San Francisco, Calif., January 16, 1998.

Jacoby, B. *Service-learning in Higher Education: Concepts and Practices.* San Francisco: Jossey-Bass, 1996.

Johnson, D. W., Johnson, R. T., and Smith, K. A. "Academic Controversy: Enriching College Instruction Through Intellectual Conflict." *ASHE-ERIC Higher Education Report,* 1996, *25* (3). Washington, D.C.: The George Washington University, Graduate School of Education and Human Development, 1996.

Kanoy, K. W., Bruhn, W., and Woodson, J. "Effects of a First-year Living and Learning Residence Hall on Retention and Academic Performance." *Journal of the Freshman Year Experience and Students in Transition,* 1996, *8* (1), 7–23.

Kuh, G. D., and others. "Student Learning Outside the Classroom: Transcending Artificial Boundaries." *ERIC Digest.* Washington, D.C.: The George Washington University, Graduate School of Education and Human Development, 1994.

Levine, A., and Cureton, J. "Collegiate Life: An Obituary." *Change: The Magazine of Higher Learning,* 1998, *30* (3), 12–17.

Levine, J., and Tompkins, D. "Making Learning Communities Work: Seven Lessons from Temple University." *AAHE Bulletin,* 1996, *48* (10), 3–6.

Luce, J., and others (eds.). *Combining Service and Learning. A Resourcebook for Community and Public Service.* Raleigh, N.C.: National Society for Internships and Experiential Education, 1990.

Maylath, B. *With Fits and Starts: How Collaborative Learning Fares in the Hierarchical, Authoritarian University,* 1991. (ED 339 031)

McGregory, J. "There Are Other Ways to Get Happy." *African American Urban Folklore.* Working papers # 2, Philadelphia, Pa.: Philadelphia Folklore Project, 1989.

Nettles, M. T., Thoeney, A. R., and Gosman, E. J. "Comparative and Predictive Analysis of Black and White Students' College Achievement Experiences." In C. Turner and others (eds.), *Racial and Ethnic Diversity in Higher Education.* Needham Heights, Mass.: Simon and Schuster, 1996, pp. 247–268.

O'Donnell, J. L. "Tools for Teaching: Personal Encounters in Cyberspace." *The Chronicle of Higher Education,* February 13, 1998, p. B7.

Priestley, W. J., and others. "Science Laboratory Instruction: Summary of Findings and Implications From Four Companion Studies." Paper presented at the annual meeting of the National Association for Research in Science Teaching, Oak Brook, Ill., March, 1997.

Ratcliff, J. L., and others. "Realizing the Potential: Improving Post-Secondary Teaching, Learning, and Assessment." University Park, Pa.: National Center on Post-Secondary Teaching, Learning, and Assessment, 1996.

Rau, W., and Heyl, B. S. "Humanizing the College Classroom: Collaborative Learning and Social Organization Among Students." *Teaching Sociology,* 1990, 18 (2), 141–155.

Schein, H. K., and Bowers, P. M. "Using Living/Learning Centers to Provide Integrated Campus Services for Freshmen." *Journal of the Freshman Year Experience,* 1992, 4 (1), 59–77.

Schroeder, C. C., and Mable, P. *Realizing the Educational Potential of Residence Halls.* San Francisco: Jossey-Bass, 1994.

Schultz, J. "Voice, Image, and Idea: The Use of Non-verbal Perception in the Development of Extended Discourse." Paper presented at the 14th Annual Meeting of the Conference on College Composition and Communications, St. Louis, Mo., March 17–19, 1988.

Smith, B. L. "Taking Structure Seriously: The Learning Community Model." *Liberal Education,* 1991, 77 (2), 42–48.

Smith, D., and others. *Diversity Works: The Emerging Picture of Student Benefits.* Washington, D.C.: American Association of Colleges and Universities, 1994.

Smith, T. B. (ed.). *Gateways: Residential Colleges and the Freshman Year Experience.* The Freshman Year Experience Monograph Series, 14. Columbia: University of South Carolina Press, 1993.

Stanton, G. C., and others. "Effects of Distance Learning on Student Outcomes in General Education Courses." *Journal on Excellence in College Teaching,* 1995, 6 (2), 131–144.

Stinson, S. "Dorm for Women Science, Math Majors Opens on Rutgers Campus." *Chemical and Engineering News,* 1990, 68 (8), 26–27.

Terenzini, P. T. *Influences Affecting the Development of Students' Critical Thinking Skills.* University Park, Pa.: National Center on Post-Secondary Teaching, Learning, and Assessment, 1993.

Terenzini, P. T., and others. "The Transition to College: Diverse Students, Diverse Stories." In F. K. Stage and others (eds.), *College Students: The Evolving Nature of Research.* Needham Heights, Mass.: Simon and Schuster, 1996, pp. 54–65.

Tinto, V., and Goodsell, A. G. *A Longitudinal Study of Learning Communities at LaGuardia Community College.* University Park, Pa.: National Center on Post-Secondary Teaching, Learning, and Assessment, 1995.

Tinto, V., and Russo, P. "Coordinated Studies Programs: Their Effect on Student Involvement at a Community College." *Community College Review,* 1994, 22 (2), 16–25.

Warren, K., and others (eds.). *The Theory of Experiential Education. A Collection of Articles Addressing the Historical, Philosophical, Social, and Psychological Foundations of Experiential Education.* Dubuque, Iowa: Kendall/Hunt Publishing Co., 1995.

ADRIANNA J. KEZAR is assistant professor of higher education at George Washington University and director of the ERIC Clearinghouse on Higher Education.

Traditional models for developing the whole student no longer serve the diverse population currently pursuing higher education. A new philosophy that focuses on the partnership between student affairs professionals and faculty is necessary to further student development.

Developing the Whole Student: The Collegiate Ideal

Lisa E. Wolf-Wendel, Marti Ruel

American higher education has long operated under the assumption that it can positively affect the growth and development of its students. This belief, as expressed by Bowen (1977), assumes that academic "environments [are] calculated to bring about desired change in people" and that colleges are "places of stirring, catalysts to help people find their unique ways" (Bowen, p. 15). It is clear that the domain of influence in American higher education has never been focused exclusively on the intellect. Rather, one of the major purposes of American higher education is to develop the whole person. In this chapter, we trace the development of this purpose and suggest how theories of student development framed in terms of developing the whole person are limited when applied to an increasingly diverse student population.

The colonial colleges were concerned with fostering the intellectual, religious, and moral development of students (Lucas, 1994). In the 1880s, American colleges continued to rally around the notion of not only educating the student's intellect, but also helping the student to understand "class responsibility, religion, property, and unhurried change" (Rudolph, 1977, p. 174). By the turn of the century, American higher education had grown more complex and programs of study more specialized, with many faculty becoming engaged in the triple demands of teaching, research, and service. With these increasing faculty responsibilities along with both the increasing number and heterogeneity of students, the task of developing the whole person shifted from being the exclusive domain of the faculty to becoming the primary responsibility of student personnel administrators (Appleton, Briggs, and Rhatigan, 1978).

For student affairs administrators, the commitment to educating the whole person has been augmented and reinforced over the years. In 1937, the American Council on Education published the first "Student Personnel Point of View." Among other points, this treatise emphasized the importance of educating the "student as a whole."

> It is the task of colleges and universities to vitalize this and other educational purposes so as to assist the student in developing to the limits of his potentialities and in making his contribution to the betterment of society. . . . This philosophy imposes upon educational institutions the obligation to consider . . . the development of the student as a person rather than . . . his intellectual training alone.

These beliefs were reaffirmed in 1949, when a revised "Student Personnel Point of View Statement" was published. In light of U.S. involvement in World War II, this new statement emphasized the need for higher education to foster education for democracy, to enhance global understanding, and to help students gain the skills to solve social problems. The 1949 statement asserts:

> The development of students as whole persons interacting in social situations is the central concern of student personnel work. . . . The concept of education is broadened to include attention to the student's well-rounded development—physically, socially, emotionally and spiritually, as well as intellectually. The student is thought of as a responsible participant in his own development and not as a passive recipient.

Subsequent documents written by student affairs professionals also emphasize the importance of educating the whole student. The 1974 statement affirms that in higher education "cognitive mastery of knowledge should be integrated with the development of persons along with cultural awareness, skills, and community responsibility." Similarly, the 1984 statement asserts that student development is grounded in "the dignity and worth of each person; the uniqueness of each person, and the opportunity for each person to realize his or her fullest potential." In 1997, the National Association of Student Personnel Administrators and the American College Personnel Association issued a statement of *Principles of Good Practice for Student Affairs.* According to this statement:

> Our beliefs about higher education serve as the foundation for our commitment to the development of 'the whole person;' our collective professional values are derived from that commitment. Values evident across the history of student affairs work include an acceptance and appreciation of individual differences; lifelong learning; education for effective citizenship; student responsibility; ongoing assessment of learning and performance (students' and our own); plural-

ism and multiculturalism; ethical and reflective student affairs practice; supporting and meeting the needs of students as individuals and in groups; and freedom of expression with civility.

Ways We Educate the Whole Person

Toward the goal of educating the whole person, academic institutions, mostly under the auspices of student affairs professionals, have engaged in the creation and sponsorship of a variety of activities. Such activities include, to name a few, new student orientation, residence hall programming, peer mentor programs, student governance, student clubs, Greek life, career and personal counseling, on-campus work opportunities, and community service activities. At the core of the student affairs movement are several theories that guide the development of such activities. While an examination of all of the relevant theories is not possible in this chapter, a brief look at three of the core theories illuminates some of the ways that American higher education has attempted to develop the whole person. Limitations of these theories, in terms of how we can use them to develop all students, are also discussed.

One core hypothesis is Chickering's theory of human development, initially developed in 1969 and revised in 1993. Broadly speaking, Chickering and Reisser (1993) suggest seven vectors of development, or seven "crises," that students typically face and ideally resolve during college. These vectors include: (1) developing competence, (2) managing emotions, (3) moving through autonomy towards interdependence, (4) developing mature relationships, (5) establishing identity, (6) developing purpose, and (7) developing integrity. Resolution of these crises is often facilitated by the collegiate environment. More specifically, through a combination of challenge and support, student affairs professionals help students to work through these crises towards the goal of developing more "awareness, skill, confidence, complexity, stability, and integration" (p. 34).

Chickering's theory is influential in American higher education and can be seen, for example, within residence hall activities and programming, peer mentor programs, and career and personal counseling centers. Chickering's theory is most easily applied to traditional-aged, residential students (Bean and Metzner, 1996). While Chickering and Reisser (1993) make an attempt to explain the relevance of their model to older students, the application of the theory does not always translate into good practice for students who are non-traditional. That Chickering's theory best explains traditional students is not surprising given that most of the psychologically-based developmental theories are founded on studies of mainstream college students (Stage, 1996).

Another guiding model for developing the whole person is Astin's involvement theory, which suggests that the amount of physical and psychological energy that a student devotes to the academic experience is positively related to the impact of college on that student (Astin, 1977, p. 134). The theory is similar to "effort" or "time on task," and traditional interpretations of the theory put the onus on students to supply and expend the "energy" towards their academic experience. Involvement theory, which has been widely tested, hypothesizes that the more involved a student is in the collegiate experience, the more positive outcomes that student will reap from that experience (see for example, Astin, 1977; Astin, 1993; Pascarella and Terenzini, 1991).

It is the influence of Astin's theory that encourages institutions of American higher education to invest resources in an array of on-campus activities. Involvement theory is behind our belief that the more opportunities we provide to our students, the more positive the impact of the college experience. Involvement theory is most typically applied to and measured by involvement in on-campus activities. As a result, those who benefit the most from involvement are traditional-aged, residential students who fit the model of student body president, resident advisor, and on-campus newspaper editor, to name a few. Involvement typically presumes that college activities, academic and social, are the main priority in students' lives. Thus, application of involvement theory does not easily take into account the diverse backgrounds, needs, and external responsibilities of all of today's students. For example, given the financial reality that exists on most college campuses, students who work, especially off-campus, are potentially excluded from the benefits of guided involvement. Working students are just one group who potentially become excluded from being developed fully when campuses focus resources solely on traditional definitions of involvement.

Tinto's (1987) theory of integration is connected to Astin's notion of involvement. Tinto's theory suggests that students are influenced by interactions with the structures and members of the academic and social systems of the college. The theory, which is aimed at explaining attrition, explains that the more "integrated" students are with the academic and social community, the more likely they are to remain enrolled. According to Pascarella and Terenzini, integration, in this context, refers to the "extent to which the individual shares the normative attitudes and values of peers and faculty in the institution and abides by the formal and informal structural requirements for membership in that community" (1991, pp. 51, 53). Two examples of how student affairs professionals use Tinto's theory to increase student retention are the admissions process (attempting to admit those students who best fit with the university profile of student success) and new student orientation (introducing the norms, expectations, and traditions of the college up-front to new students). In response to Tinto's theory, Tierney argued that the underlying goal of the theory of academic and social integration is for individuals (students) to adapt to the system "in order to achieve full development in society" (1996, p. 282). In other words, students must assimilate to the norms of the institution, which most often reflect the norms of the dominant society. If one accepts Tierney's critique of Tinto's theory, one can easily presume that individuals who are not members of the dominant culture will have a more difficult time achieving "total development." This is a potential limitation of this theory.

While these are not the only theories that guide practice, theories developed by Chickering, Astin, and Tinto could be described as foundational to the activities of student personnel administrators in the goal of developing the whole student. These theories encourage American higher education to maintain its residential communities as places where students are compelled to become involved and to be active agents in their own development. As has been pointed out, however, these theories "work best" when applied to students who are part of the mainstream typified by being on-campus, full-time, academically-focused, and self-motivated. This leads us to question whether all of today's students are in a position to benefit equally from the application of these theories. Do we holistically develop all of our students?

Students We Expect to Educate

Underlying the belief in our ability to develop the whole student is a belief that certain students possess characteristics that make them open to our influence. Faculty at the University of Kansas recently were asked, "In your opinion, what kinds of college students do you expect to teach?" This non-scientific poll of current faculty was replicated by posing a similar question to a class of master's students in the University of Kansas School of Education's Higher Education degree program. The master's degree students were asked "What kind of students do you expect to work with in your role as a student affairs professional?" Responses from both groups were similar. The following generalized characteristics emerged. Students are expected to be:

- traditional-aged, with no dependents (spouses or children);
- enrolled full-time;
- academically able to succeed and prepared for the college curriculum;
- self-motivated to be in college, to learn, and to immerse themselves in the learning community;
- open both to learning new things and to experiencing differences in others;
- self-directed, able, and prepared to select their academic degree program;
- capable of goal-setting and of taking responsibility for seeking help when they require assistance or support;
- supported financially from either the family or the federal financial aid programs, with relatively few, if any, financial concerns.

These characteristics are the same set of qualities or traits that institutions of higher education, both public and private, seek to attract to their institutions. It seems that we are all chasing those students who we think are most able to succeed. We want these students to matriculate because, from a faculty and administrative perspective, it is these students whom we can most easily develop as whole persons using theories such as those proposed by Chickering,

Astin, and Tinto. Frequently, it is the students who have these characteristics that we profile in our view books and press releases as success stories to demonstrate institutional excellence, vitality, and viability.

The characteristics of entering freshmen and exiting seniors are transformed and translated into college rankings and published in various magazines and college selection materials for general consumer use without regard to the validity and reliability of the criteria used to lay claim to such excellence. Institutions of higher education are quick to accept the accolades of positive rankings. They are equally quick to deny the validity of those rankings that are less than positive. This self-promotion and self-aggrandizement creates a gap between the type of students faculty and administrators *expect* to have at their institutions and the students they actually have before them. This gap becomes more defined as we compare the conceptual set of characteristics against the actual characteristics of today's college students.

Students We Actually Have

Compared to college students in the past, today's undergraduates are more likely to be older (over age twenty-four), to be from diverse economic and cultural backgrounds, to be in debt, to work, and to have external responsibilities beyond their academic pursuits. Specifically, recent statistics indicate that eighteen- to twenty-four year old high school graduates enrolled in college comprise only 42 percent of all students who are attending institutions of higher education (Chait, 1998). The other 58 percent, older college students, are more likely than their younger counterparts to be married with dependents. Forty-three percent of students attend part-time, a proportion that continues to grow. Significant variations exist in the economic backgrounds of students, with 45 percent of those enrolled in four-year institutions receiving some form of financial assistance; 36 percent of these same students receive their assistance in the form of loans (Chronicle of Higher Education, 1997/1998). A majority of students work while they attend college. According to the 1998 results of the freshman survey conducted by the Higher Education Research Institute (HERI), of those who expect to work while enrolled, approximately 39 percent expect to work more than sixteen hours a week (HERI, 1998). Further, the HERI survey indicated that 16 percent of college freshmen indicated that they are not sure they will have enough money to complete college. Adding to the diversity within American higher education are the 29 percent of college students who are ethnic minorities or international students. Further, women constitute over 50 percent of current undergraduates in the United States (HERI, 1998).

According to the most recent report from HERI, greater numbers of students are coming to college campuses more troubled than ever before, not only from the impact of familial problems (26 percent are from divorced families) but also from other personal problems such as substance abuse. Today's students have been labeled less academically prepared than previous generations of students (see for example, Bennett, 1992; Bloom, 1987; D'Souza, 1991). The HERI survey indicates that 11 percent of 1998 freshmen stated they needed remediation in English, 27 percent stated they needed mathematics remediation and 11 percent claimed they needed remediation in social studies. Despite seemingly poor academic preparation, college students are studying less than ever before—only 34 percent of freshmen study at least six hours a week, down from 56 percent who studied that much ten years ago (HERI, 1998). At the same time, it appears that students want high grades (above a B) for low return of effort (Levine and Cureton, 1998). Looking to the future, today's college students know that their social mobility is tied directly to a college education and that if they can graduate they will earn almost twice as much as those with only a high school education (Levine and Cureton, 1998). Their goal is social mobility.

It is important for us in American higher education to remember that every college student is unique. The essence of these students is not easily captured in a demographic snapshot. In addition, the purpose of this sketch of today's college students is not to demonstrate that students are worse than ever before. College students have never matched academia's expectations of what they should be. Helen Lefkowitz Horowitz indicated in her book, *Campus Life* (1987) that, "anger had been the characteristic mode of college professors since the late eighteenthth century" (p. xi). Perhaps the anger stems from the fact that faculty's expectations of who students are is not reality. As an example, in 1893, President Taylor of Vassar observed from the faculty point of view, "one is obliged to suspect, at times, that the student comes to be regarded as a mere disturber of ideal schemes, and as a disquieting element in what, without him, might be a fairly pleasant life" (Veysey, 1965, p. 339). Today, as in the past, higher education alleges that students have become "disengaged" (Marchese, 1998). But, given the gap that historically has existed between what faculty and administrators expect and who the real college students are, perhaps one should ask, "Have we ever fully engaged the majority of students in our learning communities?" Rather than sounding an alarm, we believe the fact that today's students represent a greater cross-section of American culture strengthens the mission of higher education and provides more opportunities to develop the whole person.

New Directions for Educating the Whole Student

Given who students are, should American higher education abandon its goal of educating the whole student? Our answer to this question is an emphatic "no!" However, current practices alone will not further our goal. Educating the whole student calls not only for new approaches to established theory, but also for the creation of new theory. We do not have all the answers to this conundrum; but our reading of the situation, guided by some great thinkers in our field, suggests some areas that might help American higher education to make progress in developing the whole student.

A recent statement by the American College Personnel Association titled, *The Student Learning Imperative,* calls for student affairs professionals to engage more directly and cooperatively with academic staff to foster student learning, broadly defined (1994). It suggests that by emphasizing student development, student affairs professionals have taken as their domain the "co-curriculum, student activities, residential life, affective or personal development." At the same time, the academic staff has taken sole responsibility for "learning," which occurs in the formal curriculum in classrooms. This split, the statement argues, is unnecessary, as "the concepts of 'learning,' 'personal development,' and 'student development' are inextricably intertwined and inseparable." Kuh and Banta (1998) echo the call for cooperation between student affairs and academic affairs. "A faculty cannot by itself accomplish the college's objectives for students' intellectual and personal development; it needs the cooperation of others who work with students where students spend the majority of their time—in employment settings, playing fields, living quarters, and so on" (p. 41). We concur.

One area that requires immediate cooperation within institutions of higher education is the assessment of students. While our campuses have required placement examinations in mathematics, English, and other core disciplines, many of us have failed (1) to assess students' motivation and desire to learn; (2) to understand what reason(s) students have for coming to college; and (3) to identify the challenges and barriers that students face (e.g., financial) in immersing themselves in the environment of the traditional four-year residential setting. We, both faculty and student affairs professionals, need to become more educated about who is on our campus. Assessing our students when they enter would accomplish several tasks. First, it would make faculty less frustrated that students are not as they expect them to be. Second, it would give us a starting point from which to evaluate the effect higher education has on graduates—a baseline measure. Third, assessment would allow student development activities to be designed to reach a wider range of students. Presently activities often seem best suited to the development of those students who hold such positions as resident advisor or student body president.

Kuh and Banta (1998) concur with the need for cooperation on assessment:

> By working together on assessment, faculty and student affairs professionals can broaden acceptable definitions and develop a common language of learning; accumulate institution-specific evidence linking out-of-class experiences to valued outcomes of undergraduate education; help identify complementary activities, services, and practices; and experiment with ways to realize these conditions more of the time. Most important, collaboration on assessment focuses institutional effort on student learning [p. 46].

In addition to the need for cooperation and more assessment, we believe that Astin's notion of "value-added" as explained in *Achieving Educational Excellence* (1985) is a key to educating the whole student. Astin argued that American higher education should move away from a resource definition of prestige in which an "excellent" college or university is measured by the entrance requirements of students, the financial and library resources of the institution, and the quality of faculty, as measured by their academic pedigree. American higher education, Astin argued, should move towards a talent development conception of excellence, which focuses on "changes in the student from the beginning to the end of an educational program. These changes can cover a wide range of cognitive and affective attributes" (p. 61). In other words, "the most excellent institutions are . . . those that have the greatest impact . . . on the students' knowledge and personal development" (Astin, 1985, p. 61).

As the burgeoning national rankings are taken more seriously by academic institutions, however, we seem to be moving farther away from embracing a value-added definition of institutional success. The majority of colleges and universities in the U.S. seek to elevate their status within the existing hierarchy of institutions of higher education. To this end, institutions invest resources in, for example, attracting national merit scholars or hiring Nobel prize winners. In our view, rather than investing resources to elevate one's prestige, we believe institutions should invest in developing the potential of all our students. While wholesale adoption of a value-added approach is idealistic and unlikely, we see some glimmers of hope that some institutions of higher education might move in this direction. For example, institutions of higher education such as historically black colleges and universities, tribal colleges and hispanic-serving colleges, which are typically open-admission and resource-poor, are slowly being recognized for their ability to move students from where they enter to where they should be upon graduation. Most of these institutions operate under the value-added premise. They graduate students who succeed beyond what might otherwise be expected given their pre-college admission credentials (Pavel, Inglebret, and Van De Hende, 1998; Wolf-Wendel, 1998). Looking toward these institutions as models of how to serve today's student suggests several lessons. Among these are the value of high expectations for student success and the need for a lot of individual and collective caring and support for students (Wolf-Wendel, 1994).

High academic expectations are known to be one of the key institutional traits associated with facilitating student success. In *Involving Colleges,* for example, Kuh, Schuh, and Whitt (1991) qualitatively examined how campuses foster student learning and development outside the classroom. They found that a trait common to successful institutions was the presence of faculty members who "assume that all students can learn anything, given the proper circumstances" (p. 284). High academic expectations were also found to be a defining principle at institutions that graduated high proportions of women who earned doctorates (Wolf-Wendel, 1994). One non-selective college in this study, for example, followed a value-added model of education, geared to "bring students from where they are when they enter, to where they should be when they exit." One means of achieving this goal was by repeatedly telling students that they could succeed, that they were capable, and that they could do, or be, anything they wanted to if they just kept trying. Faculty talked about not giving up on students who were having academic difficulties and reiterating the notion that as women, they were capable of achieving even in male dominated fields. The psychological theory of attribution (Kelley, 1973) supports the importance of high expectations in regard to developing the whole student. Attribution theory suggests that when one credits success to high ability, and failure to insufficient effort rather than to low ability, self-esteem is enhanced as is a willingness to approach challenging tasks.

Support or "mattering" is also a key to adopting a value-added model. Mattering, as explained by Schlossberg (1989), is the notion that within the collegiate environment, students come to believe that they matter and that peers, faculty and staff care about them. In other words, mattering suggests that students must have a sense of belonging if they are to succeed. Mattering further suggests that students must feel appreciated for who they are and what they do, if they are to grow, develop and succeed in college. "Clearly, institutions that focus on mattering and greater student involvement will be more successful in creating campuses where students are motivated to learn, where their retention is high, and ultimately, where their institutional loyalty for the short and long-term future is ensured" (Schlossberg, Lynch, and Chickering, 1989, p. 14). If institutions are able to convince students that they are capable and that they matter, it could go a long way in dealing with the imperfections students bring with them.

Conclusion

Idealism, well-focused, is a good thing. However, we believe that American higher education has invested too much energy in chasing the ideal college student and not enough energy in creating the ideal college. This chapter calls for a shift in ideology to one that places the responsibility for developing the whole student in a partnership among faculty, administrators and students. Knowing who our students are, having high expectations of them, and making them feel that they matter will help us to better develop the whole student.

> It is the professional duty of faculty and the administrators . . . to show that they
> care, they teach, and the students who trust them, grow, learn and develop. . . .
> Really educating undergraduate students in a coherent, purposeful, authentic,
> and durable way is the heart of the higher education business [Leslie and Fretwell,
> 1996, pp. 287, 285].

References

American College Personnel Association. *A Student Development Model for Student Affairs in Tomorrow's Higher Education*. Washington D.C.:, 1974.
American College Personnel Association. *The Student Learning Imperative: Lessons for Student Affairs*. Washington D.C., 1994.
American Council on Education. *Student Personnel Point of View*, Series I, *1* (3), 1–3. Washington D.C., 1937.

American Council on Education. *Student Personnel Point of View,* Series XI, *13* (13), 1–11. Washington D.C.: 1949.

Appleton, J. R., Briggs, C. M., Rhatigan, J. J. *Pieces of Eight: The Rites, Roles, and Styles of the Dean by Eight Who Have Been There.* Portland, Oreg.: NASPA Institute of Research and Development, 1978.

Astin, A. W. *Four Critical Years: Effects of College on Beliefs, Attitudes and Knowledge.* San Francisco: Jossey-Bass, 1977.

Astin, A. W. *Achieving Educational Excellence: A Critical Assessment of Priorities and Practices in Higher Education.* San Francisco: Jossey-Bass, 1985.

Astin, A. W. *What Matters in College? Four Critical Years Revisited.* San Francisco: Jossey-Bass, 1993.

Bean, J. P., and Metzner, B. S. "A Conceptual Model of Nontraditional Undergraduate Student Attrition." In Stage, F. K. and others (eds.), *College Students: The Evolving Nature of Research.* ASHE Reader Series. Needham Heights, Mass.: Simon and Schuster Custom Publishing, 1996.

Bennett, W. J. *The De-Valuing of America: The Fight for our Culture and Our Children.* New York: Summit Books, 1992.

Bloom, A. *The Closing of the American Mind: How Higher Education Has Failed Democracy and Impoverished the Souls of Today's Students.* New York: Simon and Schuster, 1987.

Bowen, H. R. *Investment in Learning: The Individual and Social Value of American Higher Education.* San Francisco: Jossey-Bass, 1977.

Chait, R. "Illusions of a leadership vacuum." *Change: The Magazine of Higher Learning,* 1998, *30* (1), 38–41.

Chickering, A. W., and Reisser, L. *Education and Identity,* (2nd ed.) San Francisco: Jossey-Bass, 1993.

Chronicle of Higher Education. *Almanac Issue.* Washington D.C., 1997/1998.

D'Souza, D. *Illiberal Education: The Politics of Race and Sex on Campus.* New York: Free Press, 1991.

Higher Education Research Institute. *1998 Freshman Data.* Chronicle of Higher Education Web Site. [http://chronicle.com]. 1998.

Horowitz, H. L. *Campus Life: Undergraduate Cultures From the End of the Eighteenth Century To The Present.* Chicago: The University of Chicago Press, 1987.

Kelley, H. E. "The processes of causal attribution." *American Psychologist,* 1973, *28* (2), 107–128.

Kuh, G. D., and Banta, T. W. "A Missing Link in Assessment: Collaboration Between Academic and Student Affairs Professionals." *Change: The Magazine of Higher Learning,* 1998, *30* (2), 40–46.

Kuh, G. D., Schuh, J. H., Whitt, E. J. and Associates. *Involving Colleges: Successful Approaches to Fostering Student Learning and Development Outside the Classroom.* San Francisco: Jossey-Bass, 1991.

Leslie, D. W., and Fretwell, E. K. *Wise Moves in Hard Times: Creating and Managing Resilient Colleges and Universities.* San Francisco: Jossey-Bass, 1996.

Levine, A., and Cureton, J. S. *When Hope and Fear Collide: A Portrait of Today's College Student.* San Francisco: Jossey-Bass, 1998.

Lucas, C. J. *American Higher Education: A History.* New York: St. Martin's Press Inc., 1994.

Marchese, T. "Disengaged students." *Change: The Magazine of Higher Learning,* 1998, *30* (2), 4.

National Association of Student Personnel Administrators and the American College Personnel Association. *Principles of Good Practice for Student Affairs.* Washington, D.C., 1997.

Pascarella, E. T., and Terenzini, P. T. *How College Affects Students: Findings and Insights from Twenty Years of Research.* San Francisco: Jossey-Bass, 1991.

Pavel, D. M., Inglebret, E., and Van De Hende, M. "Tribal Colleges." In Townsend, B. (ed.), *Community Colleges for Women and Minorities: Enabling Access to the Baccalaureate.* Westport, Conn.: Garland Press, 1998.

Rudolph, F. *Curriculum: A History of the American Undergraduate Course of Study Since 1636.* San Francisco: Jossey-Bass, 1977.

Schlossberg, N. K. "Marginality and mattering: Key issues in building community." In D. C. Roberts (ed.), *Designing Campus Activities to Foster a Sense of Community.* New Directions for Student Services. no. 48. San Francisco: Jossey-Bass, 1989.

Schlossberg, N. K., Lynch, A. Q., and Chickering, A. W. *Improving Higher Education Environments for Adults: Response Programs and Services from Entry to Departure.* San Francisco: Jossey-Bass, 1989.

Stage, F. K. "College outcomes and student development: Filling the gaps." In Stage, F. K. and others (eds.), *College Students: The Evolving Nature of Research.* ASHE Reader Series. Needham Heights, Mass.: Simon and Schuster Custom Publishing, 1996.

Tierney, W. G. "An Anthropological Analysis of Student Participation in College." In Stage, F. and others (eds.), *College Students: The Evolving Nature of Research.* ASHE Reader Series. New York: Simon and Schuster Custom Publishing, 1996.

Tinto, V. *Leaving College: Rethinking the Causes and Cures of Student Attrition.* Chicago: University of Chicago Press, 1987.

Veysey, L. R. *The Emergence of the American University.* Chicago: University of Chicago Press, 1965.

Wolf-Wendel, L. E. "The Baccalaureate Origins of Successful African American, Latina, and European American Women." Paper presented at the Association for the Study of Higher Education Annual Meeting, Tucson, Ariz., November, 1994.

Wolf-Wendel, L. E. "Models of Excellence: The Baccalaureate Origins of Successful African American, European American and Hispanic Women." *Journal of Higher Education,* 1998, *69* (2), 144–172.

LISA E. WOLF-WENDEL is assistant professor of higher education at the University of Kansas.

MARTI RUEL is former associate vice chancellor of student affairs at the University of Kansas.

The traditional collegiate ideal is institutionalized on many campuses through the structure and the types of services offered by student affairs units. In order to change the collegiate ideal to represent a more inclusive environment, student affairs professionals must examine their policies and procedures and make changes that will help meet the developmental needs of nontraditional students.

The Student Affairs Establishment and the Institutionalization of the Collegiate Ideal

Anna M. Ortiz

In many ways, the rise of the collegiate ideal created the profession of student affairs. The components of student life central to student affairs units (for example, athletics, Greek social organizations, student organizations, residential living) are what contribute to an individual's sense of identification with a college. These were all alive before the emergence of deans of men and women. Since the early development of student affairs administration, the collegiate ideal and institutional identification have grown in scope, both in terms of services and activities. They have also increased in importance to both our theoretical and practical understandings of student development and student success. This is in part because of a conscious effort within the student affairs field to align its services and activities with the theoretical underpinnings of psycho-social developmental theory (Chickering, 1993; Perry, 1970) and in part because of an increase in the study of the impact of college upon students (Feldman and Newcomb, 1969).

In many cases a student's ability to identify with his or her college is key to student retention and achievement, and ultimately institutional persistence and livelihood. Thus, the collegiate ideal is critical to both student and institutional success. This chapter discusses the extent to which the collegiate ideal has been accepted as necessary for both students and institutions in a climate where higher education is facing challenges about mission and outcomes. The idea of "place" in post-secondary education is changing due to technology and student need. With that change in mind, this chapter explores the ways in which student affairs units support the collegiate ideal through the institutionalization of the services and activities that create such an ideal on campuses. Finally, the utility of the institutionalized collegiate ideal will be explored bearing in mind that a changed student population, once on the horizon, is now in our backyard.

I come to this consideration of the benefits and utility of the collegiate ideal from several perspectives. As a graduate of three universities with strong identities, I have experienced the power of the collegiate ideal to shape my college experiences and my own memories of college. As a former student affairs administrator, I have experienced being an instrument of the continuing social construction of the collegiate ideal, strongly believing in its benefits to all college students. Now, as a professor teaching and mentoring future student affairs practitioners, I experience the power of the collegiate ideal in a different way. My attempts to broaden the perspectives of my students, in the hope of making them more inclusive, transformative leaders, are often thwarted by their own strong identification with the collegiate ideal and their near blind faith that uniform identification with its elements is central to student growth, persistence, and success on college campuses.

There has long been a working assumption that all students and all academic communities benefit from a traditional notion of the collegiate ideal, but to what extent is this true? Given this assumption, is it possible for student affairs bureaucracies to transfer the benefits of the collegiate ideal to those traditionally excluded from it for reasons such as age, ethnicity, or ability? This tension between what is accepted as the norm for success at college and what is needed for all students to be equal participants and beneficiaries in the college environment must be adjusted in order for diverse students to develop a strong identification with their institution.

The Collegiate Ideal as Campus Culture

The images that are uniquely collegiate—and that are found nowhere else in our society—bring a sense of fondness, pride, and yearning in those who have developed an identification with the mystique of college. Football game tailgates, sunny days on the quad, residence halls with two people sharing a space too small for one, seniors dressed in brand new blue suits on their way to an interview, and evidence of a good practical joke all bring to mind precious memories of college years. We remember a time in our lives where intellectual and social pursuits were our primary objectives. Curiously, we often think of college in this way, regardless of our own memories of our own college experiences. The ability of the collegiate ideal to "implant" memories that may not be our own is a tribute to the socially constructed, self-perpetuating power of the ideal and the control it exerts in higher education.

The institutionalized collegiate ideal resembles what scholars have defined as campus culture. Institutional history, mission, physical artifacts and settings, norms, traditions, values, practices, beliefs, and assumptions that guide individual and group behavior are all components of the college campus culture

(Kuh and Hall, 1993). Manning (1993) brings the definition of campus culture closer to the image of the collegiate ideal by discussing the role of buildings, place, ceremonies, documents, sagas, rituals or rites of passage, and language in institutional culture. While each campus has unique expressions of campus culture, an overall picture of a shared college campus culture—a collegiate ideal—exists on campuses nationwide.

When a campus does not fit the collegiate ideal because it has a campus culture different from the norm, we perceive that institution as being different or missing "something." Somehow an institution that lacks our collective notion of the collegiate ideal is considered "less than" more prestigious institutions that have captured the popular imagination. In many ways, our collective ignorance about what happens on these campuses creates the assumption that they lack the rich sense of history or the traditions that exist on campuses with well-defined, expected cultures. Furthermore, we assume that they lack the potential to develop well-defined, expected cultures or surrogates of them. The landmark study *Involving Colleges* (Kuh, Schuh, Witt, and associates, 1991) describes exemplary institutions where the collegiate ideal does exist in a variety of settings and missions. Despite evidence of the occurrence of this ideal culture on commuter campuses or at special population colleges, the reader continues to feel that they are merely exceptions to the rule. The institutionalization of the collegiate ideal, then, serves as a "yardstick" by which all colleges and universities are measured. The ability of the collegiate ideal to define the essence of what is good and right in higher education gives testimony to the power of the ideal and the place it holds in America's collective psyche. The collegiate ideal prescribes what college should be, how college students should act, and how the worth of an institution is measured.

The Benefits of the Collegiate Ideal

In a time when there is a great deal of criticism directed at American colleges and universities and at our ability to transform our institutions into places that are inclusive and representative of a diverse student population, it is often easy to be critical of the collegiate ideal. There are, however, benefits to the collegiate ideal, both for institutions and for students, that we should not overlook. When a large segment of any organization's constituency identifies strongly with the culture, purposes, and goals of that organization, the organization benefits in many ways. In a college setting, identification with the college leads to increased retention of both employees and students (Tinto, 1993). Where there is a strong sense of community, pride, and prestige, employees remain despite employment options with higher wages. Indeed, the notion of college as a place where civility exists, where jobs are often secure, and where there are benefits that are not available elsewhere (for example, tuition and cultural events), creates an ideal work environment. Many student affairs staff (and staff in other units) are graduates of the college where they are employed. Institutions, in essence, create a readily available pool of workers, generated annually, who are already trained in the culture and ways of the institution. More importantly, this pool of potential staff comes with a characteristic many in industry covet: a strong, positive identification with the organization. Additionally, in institutions where the collegiate ideal is strong, the institution's reputation and history act like a magnet, bringing the best and brightest to its grounds. Because the general public continues to evaluate the effectiveness of colleges and universities based on their ability to graduate bright students and attract talented faculty, a strong collegiate ideal acts as a self-perpetuating marketing tool.

When the culture of a college or university matches the collective ideal about college life, students are more likely to identify with the institution. In terms of fund raising and development, this is a valuable asset. For years, annual giving campaigns have employed student workers to solicit donations from alumni. A common strategy used by these young "salespeople" is to quickly get the potential donor to identify with his or her college experiences (Miller, Newman, and Seagren, 1994). When the student finds a "hit," an activity or experience the potential donor had at the institution, the student works to bring the donor back to that "place" on campus in the hope of conjuring up pleasant memories that will put the donor in a giving mood. Student callers ask alumni where they lived on campus, what activities they participated in, whether or not they were members of Greek letter organizations, or if they may have held leadership positions. Research has shown that the alumni who have been involved, even minimally, in student activities are more likely to donate to the institution (Webb, 1993). I have witnessed how skilled these callers are at taking me back to my alma maters. Their ability to conjure up my image of the collegiate ideal guarantees a donation.

Similar strategies are used in larger-scale development campaigns. External funding for research or capital improvements is often secured during a "courtship" where development personnel help foundations or benefactors connect to their particular institution. Although these folks may be less likely to be drawn to give to a college or university based on the factors that motivate alumni, elements of the collegiate ideal are used to help these constituents see the value their contribution may have at an already strong institution. Foundations and benefactors have been funding such initiatives as first-year education programs, campus community enhancement, and faculty engagement in the education of undergraduates—all of which may be easily linked to the notion of a collegiate ideal.

Traditional college students are the ones who, research indicates, get the most out of college, benefitting the most from the collegiate ideal. Tinto (1993) and Astin (1993) both show that involvement with the academic institution—both academic and social—is critical for student success and persistence. Astin (1993) demonstrates how elements of the collegiate ideal benefit students. Living away from home significantly contributes to students' satisfaction with student life and college, leadership and interpersonal skills, an increase in cultural awareness, and the likelihood that students say they would attend the same college again. Living in a residence hall leads to increased graduation rates, satisfaction with faculty, and a willingness to re-enroll in the same college. Peer group effects—the impact of fellow students on the individual—lead to increased leadership abilities, academic development (problem solving skills, preparation for graduate or professional school, and general knowledge), grade point average, and academic honors. Interaction with faculty also had positive effects, such as satisfaction with instruction, increased grade point average, degree attainment, graduate school attendance, and the awarding of honors at graduation. In short, living in residence, interacting with faculty, and being involved with one's peers are all a part of the image that is the collegiate ideal.

The collegiate ideal also fulfills a psychological need for students. Part of the reason we can conceive of a nationwide student culture is that students, regardless of where they find themselves, face the same basic challenges. If they are traditionally aged students, they choose majors, become independent, and adjust to a new place filled with new people (Love, Jacobs, Boschini, and Hardy, 1993). They are very much in a classic "developmental crisis." Erikson (1963) posited that in each new stage of human development a person experiences a crisis that is resolved by the accomplishment of the "task" of that particular stage. Choosing majors and becoming independent are characteristic of Erikson's stage of identity versus identity diffusion. If a developmental task is not resolved, then the person suffers recurrences of this crisis throughout his or her lifetime. College is the time and place for traditionally aged students to resolve this identity conflict. The institutionalization of the collegiate ideal creates an environment that nurtures exploration of possibilities by making indecision, risk taking, and the luxury of time a norm in the college culture. Those late night discussions, internships, faculty contact, and diverse student activities and organizations all contribute to the exploration and identity development process.

The notions of challenge and support in developmental schemes (Sanford, 1962) also point to the utility of the collegiate ideal in the lives of students. Sanford's "theory" tells us that in a world of challenges, students need supportive environments, people, and experiences in order to meet and conquer these challenges. The existence of a collegiate environment acts as a support mechanism for students at a time in their lives when the challenges they face have the very distinct possibility of overwhelming their ability to complete a college education and lead a productive life. Student affairs functions were created specifically to support and guide students in skills and abilities needed for adult living. Orientation, career development and placement, residence life, and counseling centers all have fundamental missions to support students at this time. Also institutionalized is the "play" necessary to offset the gravity of making decisions that have a lifetime impact.

It may be argued that the notion of the collegiate ideal is necessary for the effectiveness of colleges and universities. The collegiate ideal, indeed, may be a good thing. The culture and environment it creates on campuses make campuses desirable places to work. The rich sense of identity it gives an institution helps students more easily identify with the college, which leads to student involvement and retention. The special place colleges hold in American culture enhances institutions' ability to secure necessary funding. The collegiate ideal also builds a set of expectations for students (and others) about the purpose of a college education that makes the psycho-social and affective development of students (in addition to intellectual pursuits) important goals of college.

Institutionalizing the Collegiate Ideal Through Student Affairs

The collegiate ideal and its benefits have made an attractive organizational guide for student affairs administration as it has developed throughout this century. The structure of the affairs enterprise supports the collegiate ideal through institutionalizing many of the rituals, events, and traditions that create an image of college as place. Student affairs units such as residential life, student activities, and Greek affairs are the closest keepers of this collegiate ideal. Living in residence, being involved in clubs and organizations, and joining a fraternity or sorority are ways in which students participate in the collegiate ideal. However, we can also argue that almost any student service, including academic advising and career counseling, institutionalizes the collegiate ideal by its activities (major indecision advising, internship placement, job search assistance).

Many student affairs units continue to serve a traditional student population—white, middle-class, undergraduates, eighteen to twenty-two years of age. Those who do not—student services directly targeted toward underrepresented students, students with disabilities, or commuter students—have yet to institutionalize the notion of the collegiate ideal with their students. The collective image of college students has yet to include such diverse populations. The staffing of student affairs units provides additional evidence for the institutionalization of the collegiate ideal. Often, the very dedicated staff members in student affairs are there precisely because they so closely identified with their own institutions and the collegiate ideal, evidenced by the fact that student affairs units often employ a number of the institution's own graduates.

A number of student affairs units act as socializing agents in helping students to identify with the collegiate ideal. The image of college and the notion of place are paramount to the admissions process. When student guides in admissions offices take prospective students and their families on campus tours, they initiate the socialization process for new members of the community. Throughout the tours, the young guides pass on stories or sagas of important events and myths that surround places on campus. The language used intentionally helps the prospective student to develop a preliminary identification with the campus that will prevent that student from considering other possibilities for college attendance. Subsequent mailings, phone calls, and alumni visits to high schools continue to reinforce the perception of *this* college as ideal.

When the student arrives on campus, orientation programs and staff continue the socialization process. Orientation programs introduce students to the norms, beliefs, and expectations in both academic and co-curricular life on campus. They may learn about the many campus activities available to new students. Mock classrooms may demonstrate the level of participation and preparedness expected in the academic culture. New students participate in the annual rituals that celebrate their rite of passage onto campus. The most symbolic activities take advantage of the imagery of the collegiate ideal. A candle-lighting ceremony at the center of campus may mark "graduation" from orientation. Residence life then assumes the "torch" in the creation of a student's identification with the collegiate ideal. "Veterans" of university life quickly let the new students know what part of orientation is "real" and what is not. They present more myths and sagas, but these are usually not fit for publication in college brochures. The popular "urban myth" of securing an automatic 4.0 GPA if one's roommate should pass on is one that is communicated to nearly every student on every residential campus sometime within the first year of college.

While it goes without saying that student affairs staff are sincere in their efforts to offer students the best, most developmental educational experiences, the idea of college as place and myth continues, and not in ways that are necessarily inclusive or otherwise beneficial. A telling example of how the institutionalization of the collegiate ideal persists is the limited success of the diversity or multicultural programming typically offered by student affairs staff throughout the year. Staff quite diligently attempt to alter the collegiate ideal to be more inclusive and representative of more experiences on campus. They restructure services to serve a more diverse student body. Workshops designed to increase cultural sensitivity and decrease racism are common in a number of student affairs functional areas. Admissions staffs work hard to recruit diverse students, thus making campuses look more diverse. However, the image of college does not change. What we see when we imagine "college" remains full of traditional symbols, activities, and students. The presence of liberalism, mainly behavioral and social, is arguably the only "diversity" allowed into the myth of college.

We have even been successful in exporting the collegiate ideal. American culture has put forward the myth of college in many television shows and motion pictures. But a variety of student affairs units have also been successful in institutionalizing its exportation. Career development and placement offices have increased the importance of the internship in a student's college career. The collegiate ideal is evident in the picture we construct of the college intern. The intern is young, motivated, and ready to take advantage of every networking opportunity available. Contacts are made and sustained based, in part, on the intern's ability to find those in his or her environment who share in the identification with the collegiate ideal. Fraternity and sorority ties help to bring the novice and expert together. Shared college activities, such as student leadership positions, can also help the student to find important and powerful allies in the work world. We have all seen the banter that takes place when two graduates of the same institution, strangers at first, come together and become fast friends.

Our international student programs have also exported the collegiate ideal abroad. The notion of the ugly American is sustained, in part, because of our students who study abroad as expatriates. The degree of their identification with the *American* collegiate ideal is so strong that at times it inhibits their ability for optimum learning in foreign settings. International students studying in the United States come with the expectations the collegiate ideal generates and, in turn, take the notion of the collegiate ideal to their homes. This helps to give the world a vision of the American collegiate ideal which includes many of the same elements of the domestic version of the vision.

Benefits for Nontraditional Students?

The institutionalization of the collegiate ideal, almost by definition, excludes nontraditional students. The image of a college student does not usually include anyone over twenty-five, students of color, commuter students, or students with disabilities. Somehow, as with institutions that lack the collegiate ideal, we consider these students to be out of the norm, and we believe the possibility that they may receive fewer benefits from college to be just a fact of life. When I raise the issue of the inability of nontraditional students to benefit from most services and activities with my class of new student affairs masters students, they take the perspective of trying to convince me that being involved and being a part of a community is also important for nontraditional students—if only nontraditional students could realize the importance. Their perspective requires the nontraditional student to "fit" into the existing collegiate ideal, whether or not it meets their needs. This perspective forces the nontraditional student into a mold that was not meant for him or her. It is a mold that does not consider unique life circumstances and denies that nontraditional students have anything to contribute that may be of value to traditional students.

Nontraditional students can benefit from the collegiate ideal, if those who manage student affairs units consider that those students are not exactly the same as the students they interact with most of the day. No one prefers to feel isolated, as if the environment around them had negated their existence. Astin (1993) found that part-time and commuter students reaped the same benefits from their college experience as full-time resident students, if they worked on campus rather than off campus. With a workforce that numbers in the thousands at many institutions, the opportunity to "plug" part-time or commuter students into the environment should be numerous. This may mean that financial aid or student employment staff lobby for students to receive wages comparable to the "outside" world. The student affairs units also need to be encouraged to employ nontraditional or commuter students, not only those students previously known to them. Campus bureaucracies may also need to revisit employment eligibility policies, parking regulations, and student health benefits to allow for full participation of part-time students, who are 41 percent of the national student body and 63 percent of students over the age of twenty-four (Chronicle of Higher Education, 1997). The hours of bureaucracies on campus also communicate to students that the only "real" students are those who are free to use campus services between 9 A.M. and 5 P.M. My current and most recent employing institutions are large, public universities whose most important student services end at 5 P.M.

Campus climates and cultures, integral to the collegiate ideal, need to be changed and expanded on most campuses in order to include students of color, older students, and students with disabilities. This has proven to be most difficult. Bureaucracies and policies are easier to change than the collective image of the collegiate ideal which lives in the minds of traditional undergraduates and student affairs staff. However, even many policies and procedures remain monolithic. It is not until the "insiders" change the rules for inclusion, that the "outsiders" will begin to feel a part of the community. Astin (1993) also shows that students, in general, incur learning outcomes from the presence of diverse students on campus. Interacting with those ethnically or racially different from oneself is related to a variety of learning outcomes, including academic achievement and overall satisfaction with college. However, do we consider what the diverse students "get" from their experiences on our campuses? With lower retention rates and lower rates of satisfaction with college attributed to students of color, we must question the benefits of the collegiate experience for these students. I would venture to speculate that the inability of the collegiate ideal to include these students is related to the inability of these students to garner the same benefits from the college experience. With white students representing increasingly less of the national student population, this is a serious issue for policy and practice. Students over the age of twenty-five also experience similar, and at times greater, difficulty. Most colleges and universities are nearly devoid of services tailored to, or even considerate of, the needs of these students. I would also speculate that the average student affairs administrator would not guess that nearly 20 percent of the national student population was over twenty-five (Chronicle of Higher Education, 1997). Even when confronted with this statistic, the administrator may think that this population is not present at her or his own institution, but is the "problem" of other institutions. It is probable that those "other" institutions are not demonstrative of the collegiate ideal. Again, they are considered less prestigious, less rigorous, "less than" our conception of the ideal institution.

Student affairs administrators find themselves in a precarious situation as keepers and perpetuators of the collegiate ideal, while simultaneously working to adapt or change institutions to be more responsive and inclusive to a wider, more diverse student population. In a recent issue of the *Chronicle of Higher Education* (February 13, 1998), two articles show that campuses are working to alter the collegiate ideal. In one case, student affairs administrators lead the way by redesigning residence halls to reflect the needs of more than first-year students (Gose, 1998). In another, the author ponders the development of community and relationships in a computer age (O'Donnell, 1998). While, in the second case, student affairs administrators are not leading the way in the development of community in this new way, they should be. Who better to reinvent campus community in a technological age? With personal development, communication skills, and relationship development as the base for many of our theoretical underpinnings, student affairs administrators are the logical forerunners in this endeavor. They are the leaders on campus who have the ability and the talent to transfer the benefits of the collegiate ideal to those who have been disenfranchised from it. The struggle student affairs personnel experience, both internally and externally, demonstrates the power of the collegiate ideal and the extent of its institutionalization in higher education. Student affairs administrators can take the collegiate ideal, which at times controls and limits their work, and can attempt to change institutions and cultures to reflect an ideal which is closer to the goals and missions of higher education. The institutionalization of a revised collegiate ideal has the potential to transfer the many benefits of the ideal to a broader range of students and institutions, and can increase the benefits to its traditional benefactors.

References

Astin, A.W. *What Matters in College? Four Critical Years Revisited.* Jossey-Bass: San Francisco, 1993.

Chronicle of Higher Education. *The Almanac of Higher Education.* Chicago: University of Chicago Press, 1997.

Chickering, A. *Education and Identity.* (2nd ed.) San Francisco: Jossey-Bass, 1993.

Erikson, E. *Childhood and Society.* (2nd ed.) New York: W. W. Norton, 1963.

Feldman, K., and Newcomb, T. *The Impact of College on Students.* San Francisco: Jossey-Bass, 1969.

Gose, B. "Colleges Invest Millions on Improvements to Keep Upperclassmen in Campus Housing." *Chronicle of Higher Education,* February 13, 1998, p. A52.

Kuh, G. D., and Hall, J. E. "Using Cultural Perspectives in Student Affairs." In G. D. Kuh (ed.), *Cultural Perspectives in Student Affairs Work.* Lanham, Md.: American College Personnel Association, 1993.

Kuh, G. D., Schuh, J. H., Whitt, E. J., and associates. *Involving Colleges: Successful Approaches to Fostering Student Learning and Development Outside the Classroom.* San Francisco: Jossey-Bass, 1991.

Love, P. G., Jacobs, B. A., Boschini, V. J., and Hardy, C. M. "Student Culture." In G. D. Kuh (ed.), *Cultural Perspectives in Student Affairs Work.* Lanham, Md.: American College Personnel Association, 1993.

Manning, K. "Properties of Institutional Culture." In G. D. Kuh (ed.), *Cultural Perspectives in Student Affairs Work.* Lanham, Md.: American College Personnel Association, 1993.

Miller, M. T., Newman, R. E., and Seagren, A. T. *Overview of Literature Related to the Study and Practice of Academic Fund Raising,* 1994. (ED 378 866)

O'Donnell, J. J. "Tools for Teaching: Personal Encounters in Cyberspace." *Chronicle of Higher Education,* Feb. 13, 1998, p. B7.

Perry, W. *Forms of Ethical Development in the College Years: A Scheme.* New York: Holt, Rinehart, and Winston, 1970.

Sanford, N. "Developmental Status of the Entering Freshman." In N. Sanford (ed.), *The American College: A Psychological and Social Interpretation of the Higher Learning.* New York: John Wiley and Sons, 1962.

Tinto, V. *Leaving College: Rethinking the Causes and Cures of Student Attrition.* Chicago: University of Chicago Press, 1993.

Webb, C. H. "The Role of Alumni Affairs in Fund Raising." In M. J. Worth (ed.), *Educational Fund Raising Principles and Practice.* Phoenix: Oryx Press, 1993.

ANNA M. ORTIZ is assistant professor of higher education at Michigan State University.

Faculty incentives are skewed away from the collegiate ideal, particularly at research universities. Is it inevitable that reasearch-oriented faculty divorce themselves from campus life, or can the incentive system be reshaped to incorporate faculty contributions to campus life?

Faculty Culture and College Life: Reshaping Incentives Toward Student Outcomes

Marilyn J. Amey

Traditionally, faculty role and workload are shaped by academic culture, including values and incentives that tend to be in large part discipline related and institutionally driven. Teaching, research, and service are the common tri-, partite "assignments" for faculty, with weights, distributions, and definitions of terms being more institutionally specific than discretely generalizable (Moore and Amey, 1993). As institutions evolve, so do the expectations held for and by faculty. As new initiatives and directions take hold, it is common to find faculty work following suit, at least as a generality. For example, an academic unit interested in increasing its national standing and prestige is likely to reflect this ambition in increased expectations for faculty-generated external research funding, publications, and national visibility. Faculty also do not maintain the same interests and levels of expertise in all three areas over the life of their career, and often negotiate greater emphasis on one area for a period of time (Baldwin, 1990).

Many come to the professoriate for altruistic reasons, and report strong motivation to remain, based on intrinsic rewards (for example, contact with students, love of teaching, intellectual curiosity [Moore and Amey, 1993]). It is also clearly demonstrated in the literature that faculty will respond in kind to those activities and behaviors for which they are reinforced either in the tenure and promotion processes or in annual evaluation for salary increases. Often, these two sets of rewards are not in concert and can even be cause for significant conflict and frustration for faculty, especially, but not exclusively, those in untenured positions.

In addition to the established norms and evaluation criteria for each discipline and each institution, there have been two competing pressures felt by faculty at research universities over the last decade or so. The first has been a perception by faculty (if not a reality in practice) that post-secondary institutions are moving toward an emphasis on research over teaching. At ratios often higher than two to one, faculty at comprehensive colleges through research universities believe that there has been a shift in focus and evaluation to favor research over teaching (Atkinson and Tuzin, 1992). Numerous studies have been conducted demonstrating both the perception of what Fairweather (1993) calls "academic drift" toward a stronger focus on research even at traditional teaching institutions such as liberal arts colleges, and the reality of the negative relationship of time spent on teaching with reward and promotion. Atkinson and Tuzin claim that the relative focus on research has not only separated faculty and undergraduate students but also estranged them.

The second major press in the last decade has been increasing pressure from legislators and the public at large to improve the quality of undergraduate education specifically, and teaching in general. The expectations are not without foundation, certainly, but they bring to light once again the paradoxical life of many faculty—the conflict between time (and often desire) spent on teaching and students, and reward systems overly oriented toward research productivity. As additional evidence of the seeming contradiction between value on undergraduate education and value of research, remember that often we encourage the buying out of teaching time to conduct research or reduced teaching loads for junior people as an effort to support their success in the academy, thus taking faculty out of contact with undergraduate students. There is also a fairly common practice to shift lower division courses to TAs instead of full-time faculty, again removing full-time faculty from direct involvement in the lives of students (Atkinson and Tuzin, 1992).

The scrutiny of undergraduate education raises a historical concern in the evaluation process—how to evaluate teaching effectively. One perspective is that emphasis on research has been a function of the more "objectified" criteria used to assess it, while teaching remains a very personally and individually constructed mix of pedagogy, philosophy, and content that others are less qualified and appropriate to judge. A similar argument could be made about the difficulty of evaluating other student-related activities such as advising, independent study and thesis work, and time spent in out-of-class student activities, whether they be labeled service learning, service outreach, or student development. Regardless of the rationale, reconciliation is an ongoing tightrope walk for many. Some do not succeed in the system and move to institutions that more closely align with personal value systems; others choose to leave academe altogether; and still others find that fifty-hour weeks hardly suffice for accomplishing the myriad tasks laid before them.

It is into this turbulent faculty climate that we introduce (or more accurately, re-introduce) concern with the collegiate ideal and student development. An immediate reaction for many already struggling to manage the multiple roles is, "Who has the time?" As evidence, in a study of faculty norms related to recommendations for improving undergraduate education, two of the recommendations—faculty–student interaction and learning about students—did not garner strong normative support (Braxton, Eimers, and Bayer, 1996). Encouraging faculty–student interaction may be seen as meaning out-of-class time or time spent on non-academic matters such as affective concerns. Faculty in the Braxton, Eimers, and Bayer study tended to see their role as ensuring cognitive growth and success, and as disciplinary experts, not necessarily as affective nurturers or developmental counselors. Similarly with learning about students, Braxton, Eimers, and Bayer (1996) conclude faculty may believe this is a personal choice or decision and therefore not something needing strong normative support. If faculty do not value certain institutional foci, they will not likely act on them without provocation. In a discussion on student development, faculty will not likely become involved in the lives of students if there is no intrinsic or extrinsic reward associated with doing so. At the same time, an appropriate question seems to be, "If we are not attending to student development, why are we at an educational institution?"

Alternative Conversations on Campus

Faculty conservatives abound at research universities. These are persons who subscribe to traditional norms and expectations related to research, teaching, and service in this particular institutional environment. The idea of student development per se, in or out of the classroom, may not be held as a high priority. At the same time, a series of alternative conversations has occurred in recent years that is beginning to permeate the ivory towers and to generate enthusiasm, support, and grounded research at both institutional and national levels. These conversations are often spawned by national reports such as "An American Imperative: Higher Expectations for Higher Education," led by professional associations such as the American Association of Higher Education with its timely national conference discussions (for example, "Taking Teaching Seriously"). Other conversations are instigated by research of well-known scholars such as Thomas Angelo and Patricia Cross's work on classroom assessment (1993), George Kuh's examination of seamless learning (1996), and Robert Menges's focus on teaching and learning (1990). Of the many alternative conversations taking place today, five are briefly highlighted here as examples of attention to faculty role and responsibility in the lives and development of students, both in and out of the classroom. They focus on learning, learning communities, on-line communities, assessment, and the changing role of faculty.

Focus on Learning. At the same time that there has been increased attention given to improving the quality of undergraduate instruction (teaching), there has been a parallel discussion of the need to shift the focus to student achievement (learning). What makes this shift exciting and challenging is the overt acknowl-edgment, perhaps for the first time in many minds, that teaching and learning are not synonymous concepts. We have long debated the whys and wherefores of mea-suring effective teaching, how to reward it, and its role in the distribution of fac-ulty time. We have paid far less attention to the same questions related to student learning and learning outcomes, and essentially no attention when the questions relate to activity beyond the classroom walls. Perhaps this is because, as Menges (1990, p. 107) reminds us, "most teaching occurs in the classroom, most learning does not. Learning may occur in any setting where learners encounter the subject matter of study." As a result, faculty often choose to focus on that area over which they traditionally have jurisdiction—the formal classroom–laboratory and instruc-tion. Student affairs practitioners have long suggested the need to look beyond the formal curriculum to understand the complex learning equation, but their sug-gestions often fall on deaf ears. Yet Menges (p. 107) insists that "The job of the teacher is to be cognizant of all those settings [where learning takes place], using them to shape an environment conducive to learning. The essence of teaching is the creation of situations in which appropriate learning occurs." This is a different approach to the instructional role, one that emphasizes learning rather than teach-ing, and one that accommodates multiple settings for learning.

One of the strongest proponents of the shift from teaching to learning is Terry O'Banion, author of *A Learning College for the Twenty-First Century*. Although his institutional focus is the community college, O'Banion's message is equally provocative for consideration in the research university. O'Banion (1997) characterizes our post-secondary system as time-bound, place-bound, efficiency-bound, and role-bound. In coming to terms with our academic embeddedness and its impact on achieving real learning, we see clear evidence of O'Banion's criticism in the following:

- Course scheduling time blocks and academic calendar years are rooted in agrarian economic models and false understandings of how learning occurs [time-bound].
- "School is a place" (O'Banion, p. 12), making it difficult to envision alter-nate forms of educational delivery and even different locations for traditional delivery [place-bound].
- Reliance upon business principles and values, particularly rules and regula-tions that routinize learning processes for all learners and policies designed to make efficient what is in effect bad practice, wreak havoc on reform efforts [bureaucracy-bound].
- Teachers are the purveyors of knowledge and students are the recipients, leading logically to a teacher-centered educational experience rather than anything that reflects the needs, interests, and personal knowledge of the learner [role-bound].

O'Banion concludes that, without significant transformation of our academic organizations and a focus on learning, only minor structural changes are achieved and the status quo of teaching-centered, traditional classroom academic experiences is basically maintained.

Learning Communities. Thomas Angelo (1997) operationalizes the learning college of O'Banion and the learning-centered academic institution of the likes of Barr and Tagg (1995) into "learning communities." The communities are centers of faculty and students (and often, more inclusively, administrators, staff, and the larger community) "working collaboratively toward shared academic goals in environments in which competition is de-emphasized" (p. 3). Teachers and students are all learners and teachers; faculty become designers of learning environments and experiences, rather than transmitters of knowledge in a prescribed manner. Learning communities are not prescriptive in their design, but often have common components such as purposive groupings of students, common scheduling, significant use of collaborative/cooperative learning experiences, and a sense of integration across discipline, course boundaries, and learning environments (p. 3). When taken to a logical extension beyond two or three formal courses, what can result is a collegiate transformation where faculty and students are engaged in learning, where the "community of learners" (O'Banion, 1997) transcends traditional academic boundaries, and where undergraduate education becomes a more truly seamless learning experience. The evidence demonstrating the degree to which learning communities enhance student learning is not yet conclusive, though the results are promising (Angelo, 1997). Less evident is documentation that participation in learning communities enhances faculty learning without interjecting more negative professional consequences. This will need to be addressed in order to implant this strategy into the value system of many research university faculty, especially if they are expected to move beyond the traditional classroom.

On-Line Communities. The virtual university and the virtual classroom are in vogue today, although exact definitions seem to vary in practice from setting to setting. From instructional technology in its various configurations to something as transformational as the Western Governors University, the traditional definition of undergraduate education as students coming to campus and sitting in rows with an instructor at the front for 50–90 minutes is in transition. For many, apart from the logistical and technological questions, the burning issue is the impact on student learning and development of what is truly an alternate learning environment. There is not yet sufficient evidence about the degree to which on-line instruction and the virtual classroom increase learning outcomes for students (as opposed, perhaps, to satisfaction) and the degree to which development of such instructional environments may actually penalize faculty. Though conversations abound, recent surveys show that no more than 10 percent of faculty are doing very much with technology in the classroom (Geoghegan, 1994). For many, great concern lies in the impact of technology on the sense of community fostered through the collegiate ideal and the important relationships between faculty and students, and students and their peers in the classroom. Advocates and futurists suggest that community will not be lost but the nature and definition of it will likely change as on-line communities increase.

Critics suggest that caution be used when assessing the value of technology, because increased productivity (measured in FTE, faculty/student ratios, and cost equations) may not be equivalent to increased student learning and development (O'Banion, 1997).

Assessment. Corresponding with, and sometimes the antecedent to the discussions of a learning focus, is an increased emphasis on assessment. National accrediting agencies have been diligent in requiring institutions to posit new plans for assessing learning (as opposed to teaching) outcomes, especially over the last five years. Unlike some past efforts at changing institutional cultures, this latest accrediting effort has actively sought follow-through and a clear demonstration that campus plans are being enacted. Cross (1991), Angelo (1993), and others have been writing about classroom assessments for years, but "suddenly" their work is taking on greater importance as faculty struggle to move beyond traditional, standardized, summative assessments of teaching. Purposeful, tailored, authentic assessments took hold in the late 1980s in public schools, but seem to be making sustained appearances at colleges and universities in only the last two to three years. As Cross (1991, p. 20) suggests, "The ultimate criterion of effective teaching is effective learning." She adds, "Learning probably depends more on the behavior of students than on the performance of the teacher. . . . The purpose is to involve students actively in their own learning and to elicit from them their best learning performance."

Cross (1991) suggests a very different model of assessment than we relied on in the past for both describing faculty teaching productivity and measuring teaching effectiveness. Angelo and Cross (1993, p. 5) suggest that classroom assessment focus on three questions: What are the essential goals and knowledge that need to be taught? (teaching goals), How do you know if students are learning them? (assessment techniques), and How do you help students learn better? (informed instructional improvement). Keig and Waggoner (1994) suggest that, with a focus on learning, we are likely to have various definitions of effective teaching, definitions that are constructed with different contexts, different goals, and different objectives of desired outcomes of instruction in mind. Therefore, the answers to Angelo and Cross's questions would need to be addressed for each learning situation, in or out of the formal classroom, not set out as an a prior dictum.

There is much work to be done in changing the nature of assessment in a culture that has been dominantly teacher focused, efficiency driven, and research oriented. Time spent addressing the challenge, finding or creating appropriate learning measures and environments, and educating faculty on their role as learning assessors are work components that heretofore have not been included in typical annual evaluation criteria, yet which likely constitute substantial commitments among faculty and staff. If we are to truly move in this direction, these efforts need to be supported and rewarded appropriately.

Changing Role of Faculty. Implicit in the other descriptions of alternative discussions on campus is a changing role for faculty in the twenty-first century. Even if we acknowledge that all faculty do not excel equally in teaching, research, and service, or that they will not balance their roles equally in a constant fashion over their careers, these alternative suggestions make it clear that faculty lives will not remain static. For example, making the paradigmatic shift from a focus on teaching to one on learning is a radical departure for many. Coming to terms with a "learning facilitator" persona (O'Banion, 1997) when one has spent a career as a knowledge expert is not an easy adjustment. Collaborating with students in the design of in-class and out-of-class experiences and in the definitions of their learning is inconsistent with the way many faculty have thought about instruction and their own role as faculty. Removing place and time restrictions from the way we think about undergraduate education, thus working to reconstruct teaching load equations apart from credit hour equivalencies, in-class time requirements, and a designated number of formal courses per year, requires substantive changes in both faculty and administrative mindsets. Facing their own inhibitions about technology and concerns about its place in the undergraduate experience is only the first step in enacting on-line communities. Faculty must also begin to think very differently about the meaning of community, how it is fostered and maintained, and their role as community members rather than only as instructional activities directors. They also need to embrace the challenge of learning assessments and their role as formative assessors. Rather than seeing themselves primarily as summative evaluators who assign term grades, faculty need to re-orient themselves into a role of learning facilitator, providing regular feedback to students and adapting learning experiences to better support student achievement in and out of the classroom.

For many, these suggested changes in the role of faculty would be welcomed. They stand as overt acknowledgment of efforts already being made by some and of long-standing value systems held by others that have been unsubstantiated in the culture of the research university. For others, these changes cause greater role conflict because they suggest a potential refocusing of effort away from research and toward teaching. In reality, an institution need not prioritize its activities differently in order to achieve greater student learning outcomes. If faculty were not conducting research on classroom assessment, involving colleges, and service learning, for example, there would be no models to draw upon or documented experiences to learn from in these areas. What will be required is a willingness to take learning and development seriously in faculty assessment, and to reward activities (including scholarship on teaching and learning, academic and group advising, and other developmental out-of-class experiences) that increase student outcomes rather than allow the perpetuation of an evaluation system that effectively penalizes and ignores efforts in these areas. In the complex environment of the research university, there should be room for appropriately evaluating and rewarding excellent scholarship, excellent teaching that increases student learning, and excellent campus citizenry as it fosters student development as well as institutional governance.

Reshaping Evaluation Models and Incentives Toward Student Outcomes. Research universities are extremely tradition-bound institutions where change is often hard to accomplish. They are also places where innovative thought and practice abound, even when it is not broadly recognized. Many creative evaluation models and incentive structures already exist within pockets of research universities, or have been posited by faculty within those institutions. A few of these ideas illustrate ways in which evaluation models and incentive structures can be reshaped toward student outcomes.

Teaching. Several suggestions have already been made about how the activity of teaching may need to change in order to better support the learning outcomes of students. When we focus on learning, O'Banion advises that success comes "only when improved and expanded learning can be documented" for learners (1997, p. 60). How learning-centered instructional activities are captured in evaluation schemas is the next step in moving toward real change.

Teaching portfolios are one way of accommodating a changing teaching activity and outcome. Brought to the forefront by Seldin (1991) and his colleagues (Seldin, Annis, and Zubizarreta, 1995), teaching portfolios are an attempt to capture more richly the complexities of teaching and the teacher–learner relationship, and to describe more clearly the outcomes of that relationship. They are more elaborate and reflective than the traditional, standardized student evaluations used by most universities, and they provide a mechanism by which faculty members think through and articulate to others the meaning of their teaching. Portfolios contain samples, "not just [of] what teachers say about their practice but artifacts and examples of what they actually do" (Edgerton, Hutchings, and Quinlan, 1991, p. 4). Among these examples could easily be exemplars of student work illustrating the relationship between teaching and learning in and out of the classroom. Exemplary theses, independent student research, or service learning journals could be included, affording recognition of critical and time-consuming faculty activity outside the traditional classroom.

Portfolios also include reflective statements in which faculty describe "personal teaching philosophy, strategies, and objectives" or articulate "teaching goals for the next five years" (Seldin, 1991, p. 10). These personal statements of faculty might be adapted to include an emphasis on learning, as well as teaching, and those strategies, objectives, and future goals a faculty member sees as integral to the achievement of student learning. The reflective statements also provide an opportunity for faculty to articulate their beliefs about advising, out-of-class instructional activities, and their role in student development. Because the teaching portfolio intentionally contextualizes instruction in pedagogical contexts, it potentially captures learning needs and differences, as well as instructional adaptations, strategies, and environments far more effectively than standardized teaching evaluation criteria. All of these activities are already part of the work of faculty truly engaged in developing the whole student, but most of these go unrecorded (and therefore unrewarded) in evaluation schema that focus only on quantitative measures, head counting, and traditional learning settings.

More than 500 institutions (not all of which were research universities) used teaching portfolios in 1995 (Paulsen and Feldman, 1995). Although there is not significant empirical evidence suggesting that the use of teaching port-folios systematically increases improvement of instruction or learning, it is clear that a carefully constructed portfolio includes those elements of instruction that more clearly reflect institutional values and that allow for more careful assessment by others in a review process. A research university truly interested in reshaping evaluation criteria might be well served to consider the use of teaching portfolios that focus on achievement of student outcomes.

Research. The existence of traditionally defined research at research uni-versities does not inherently preclude faculty from becoming more actively engaged in student outcomes. At the same time, if we adhere to Boyer's (1990) re-description of scholarship, many of the scholarly activities required by fac-ulty to improve student outcomes could become accepted parts of the annual evaluation of research rather than becoming a detriment in the zero-sum time equation for faculty.

Boyer (1990) posited four aspects of scholarship: discovery, integration, application, and teaching. The latter is the most obviously applicable to this discussion, but not exclusively so. The scholarship of teaching includes the acquisition of knowledge requisite for effective teaching and an active engage-ment in the subject matter; it should also include understandings of pedago-gies and learning theories, and perhaps even a gamut of student development theories so faculty understand more fully the population with which they work. Scholarship of teaching has traditionally been assumed within the assess-ment of teaching. Scholarship of integration, and, to some extent, of applica-tion, could encompass action research activities used in classroom assessments, in "class as unit of analysis" research, and in other interventions that focus on student development.

Action research is still emerging as an acceptable form of research in many research universities, yet at its heart (when applied to the practice of teaching) is the improvement of instruction leading to increased student outcomes. Those faculty involved in action research have often found their scholarship ignored by the peer review process or considered another aspect of the teach-ing or service component. Conversely, the systematic collection and analysis of these same classroom data by someone other than the instructor of record is often lauded as high-quality and important research. Faculty cannot easily improve learning outcomes without action research and other forms of class-room inquiry. There needs to be room in the research evaluation scheme to accommodate this activity. Similar arguments might be made for action research looking at student independent research processes, advising, resi-dential living, or student organizations. Should this scholarship be undertaken to improve practice, it is often accepted in "less prestigious" practitioner jour-nals, disseminated as in-house technical reports, or evaluated as service activ-ity. Until the work becomes more accepted, there is a disincentive for faculty to pursue such critical developmental activity.

Service. Most faculty operate with the belief that service is something one needs to do to be considered a good citizen, but not something to be rewarded.

Much of the work with students in which faculty engage gets listed under service, and acknowledged with a smile or a check-mark on the evaluation criteria. Because of the amount of time and energy faculty spend in work that has characteristically been called service, recent efforts have been made to provide ways for systematically evaluating and rewarding these activities (Singleton, Burack, and Hirsch, 1997). Sandmann (1996), for example, has proposed a "service portfolio," similar to the ideas encompassed in the teaching portfolio. The service portfolio provides opportunity for faculty to submit exemplars of their work in this area as well as reflective statements illustrating the ways in which the activities presented support institutional priorities, integrate with faculty interests, research, and instruction, and have a value-added impact on the overall contribution of faculty. Work that supports student development, especially that taking place out of the classroom, could easily become a more effectively documented and assessed part of the service portfolio, thereby being recognized and valued in the evaluation process.

Conclusion

It is not inevitable that research-oriented faculty divorce themselves from students and campus life. In order for them to actively participate, however, changes need to occur in faculty culture, evaluation and reward schemata, and the types of conversations in which faculty engage on campus. The traditional tripartite roles of faculty are already being challenged by the changing collegiate enterprise, and a focus on student development adds an additional perspective to consider. Even with the challenges, change is slow to occur and slower to be embraced within the faculty value system. Fortunately, creative and future-oriented discussions are taking place, and critically important work is being done to reshape faculty priorities and reward structures. In the same way that recent efforts worked to create a supportive teaching culture, current and future efforts need to focus on creating a supportive learning and development culture that encourages faculty participation in what has long been seen as their most critical function: the development of students.

References

Angelo, T. A. "A 'Teacher's Dozen': Fourteen General, Research-based Principles for Improving Higher Learning in Our Classrooms." *AAHE Bulletin,* 1993, *45* (8), 3–7.

Angelo, T. A. "The Campus as Learning Community: Seven Promising Shifts and Seven Powerful Levers." *AAHE Bulletin,* 1997, *49* (9), 3–6.

Angelo, T. A., and Cross, K. P. *Classroom Assessment Techniques: A Handbook for College Faculty.* San Francisco: Jossey-Bass, 1993.

Atkinson, R. C., and Tuzin, D. "Equilibrium in the Research University." *Change: The Magazine of Higher Learning,* 1992, *24* (3), 20–32.

Baldwin, R. G. "Faculty Career Stages and Implications for Professional Development." In J. H. Schuster and D. W. Wheeler (eds.), *Enhancing Faculty Careers.* San Francisco: Jossey-Bass, 1990, pp. 20–40.

Barr, R. B., and Tagg, J. "From Teaching to Learning: A New Paradigm for Undergraduate Education." *Change*, 1995, *27* (6), 12–25.

Boyer, E. L. *Scholarship Reconsidered*. New York: Harper and Row, 1990.

Braxton, J. M., Eimers, M. T., and Bayer, A. E. "The Implications of Teaching Norms for the Improvement of Undergraduate Education." *The Journal of Higher Education*, 1996, *67* (6), 603–625.

Cross, K. P. "College Teaching: What Do We Know About It?" *Innovative Higher Education*, 1991, *16* (1), 7–25.

Edgerton, R., Hutchings, P., and Quinlan, K. "The Teaching Portfolio: Capturing the Scholarship in Teaching." Washington, D.C.: American Association for Higher Education, 1991. (ED 353 892)

Fairweather, J. S. *Teaching, Research, and Faculty Rewards*. University Park: Pennsylvania State University, National Center on Post-secondary Teaching, Learning, and Assessment, 1993.

Geoghegan, W. H. "Stuck at the Barricades: Can Information Technology Really Enter the Mainstream of Teaching and Learning?" *AAHE Bulletin*, 1994, *47* (1), 13–15.

Keig, L., and Waggoner, M. D. *Collaborative Peer Review: The Role of Faculty in Improving College Teaching*. ASHE-ERIC Higher Education Reports #2. Washington, D.C.: The George Washington University, School of Education and Human Development, 1994.

Kuh, G. D. "Guiding Principles for Creating Seamless Learning Environments for Undergraduates." *Journal of College Student Development*, 1996, *37* (2), 135–148.

Menges, R. J. "Using Evaluation Information to Improve Instruction." In P. Seldin (ed.), *How Administrators Can Improve Teaching*. San Francisco: Jossey-Bass, 1990, pp. 104–121.

Moore, K. M., and Amey, M. J. *Making Sense of the Dollars: The Costs and Uses of Faculty Compensation*. ASHE-ERIC Higher Education Report #5. Washington, D.C.: The George Washington University, School of Education and Human Development, 1993.

O'Banion, T. *A Learning College for the 21st Century*. Phoenix: American Association of Community Colleges/Oryx Press, 1997.

Paulsen, M. B., and Feldman, K. A. *Taking Teaching Seriously: Meeting the Challenge of Instructional Improvement*. ASHE-ERIC Higher Education Report #2. Washington, D.C.: The George Washington University, Graduate School of Education and Human Development, 1995.

Sandmann, L. (ed.). *Fulfilling Higher Education's Covenant with Society: The Emerging Outreach Agenda*. East Lansing: Michigan State University, 1996.

Seldin, P. *The Teaching Portfolio*. Bolton, Mass.: Anker, 1991.

Seldin, P., Annis, L. F., and Zubizarreta, J. "Using the Teaching Portfolio to Improve Instruction." In W. A. Wright (ed.), *Teaching Improvement Practices*. Bolton, Mass.: Anker, 1995.

Singleton, S. E., Burack, C. A., and Hirsch, D. J. "Faculty Service Enclaves." *AAHE Bulletin*, 1997, *49* (8), 3–7.

MARILYN J. AMEY *is professor of higher education at Michigan State University.*

The model of shared governance between faculty and administrators plays a vital role in our conception of the collegiate ideal. How will technological and environmental changes affect this model and consequently our notion of college?

Challenges Facing Shared Governance Within the College

Christopher C. Morphew

The American college is a uniquely complex organization. Some of this complexity is a product of the multiple and differentiated tasks that are at the heart of the college's mission. The college's primary missions of research, teaching, and service, because of their subjective nature, lend complexity to the organization's policies, practices, and structure. Yet the lack of an objective technical model for knowledge production and transmission can explain only some of the peerless nature of our college communities. A large part of what is unique about our notion of college as an organization and community can be explained by examining and describing the traditional collegial model for relationships cultivated between faculty and administrators. These relationships are a function of shared governance and play a vital role in our conception of the collegiate ideal. It is also these relationships—and thus the traditional nature of collegiate governance—that are being affected by current and foreseeable changes in the evolution of the American college. As the relationship between faculty and administrators and their respective roles within the college change, so too must our notion of the college.

This monograph portrays the American college within the context of a changing environment that may have an impact upon the existence of what we know as the collegiate ideal. Toward that end, this chapter will discuss the traditions of shared governance and the challenges that face this established means of organizing and governing the American college. As part of the discussion, the chapter will include a short historical description of how shared governance has evolved and is currently defined within the American college.

NEW DIRECTIONS FOR HIGHER EDUCATION, no. 105, Spring 1999 © Jossey-Bass Publishers

In addition, a discussion of how changes in the environment and technical cores of colleges have brought about threats to the traditional nature of shared governance will be included.

Shared Governance

The variety and complexity of the tasks performed by institutions of higher education produce an inescapable interdependence among governing board, administration, faculty, students and others. The relationship calls for adequate communication among these components, and full opportunity for appropriate joint planning and effort (AAUP, 1966, p. 1). The concept and application of shared governance is unique to colleges. The notion that faculty and administrators should share in the organizational responsibilities of their institution and have primary authority for specific areas and actions within the college is a idea tied to the nature of the college. It is an idea indicative of the fact that higher education institutions are unique organizations, requiring both administrative and scholarly expertise. Traditionally, this has been reflected in the career paths of college presidents, as most have come from the faculty ranks. Moreover, there are many areas within higher education institutions where the administrative and scholarly elements are inextricably merged (for example, department chairs). Because of the comprehensive nature of modern colleges and universities, this concept of shared governance has become more integral as specialized expertise in the areas of budgets and public relations has taken on a level of importance historically reserved for technical areas (such as teaching and research) and colleges have expanded into new realms. Sometimes, ascertaining which group—administrators or faculty—should have primary authority for these areas of the college is difficult.

In their 1996 "Statement on Government of Colleges and Universities," the American Association of University Professors (AAUP) provides a detailed breakdown of the responsibilities and authority that should be conferred upon faculty and administrators. The Statement indexes responsibilities according to whether they should be considered the responsibility of (a) the governing board; (b) administration; (c) faculty; or (d) groups with memberships from several areas of the institution. For example, the statement ascribes to the administration the responsibility for leading the institution toward jointly defined goals and for general administrative actions. Faculty, conversely, are to have responsibility for curricular areas and all matters that relate to instruction, research, and the academic preparation of students (AAUP, 1996). In their statement, the AAUP does not argue for the exclusive authority of the administration or faculty in any of these areas, however. Rather, they profess their support for shared governance, but make the point that "primary" responsibility for specific areas of institutional government exist and should be respected and protected.

Traditions of Collegiate Governance

The notion of shared governance that exists today has evolved over time as governing boards, faculty, and administrators sought authority over specific portions of their organizations. The colonial American college generally vested in its governing board and college president exclusive authority over the operations of the college. The president was placed in charge of a range of daily duties important to the college's successful operation and tended to function "as an authority unto himself" (Lucas, 1994, p. 124). This arrangement was not original to the American college. Rather, it was imported from the English collegiate model and illustrated the lack of faith college founders and trustees had in their faculty (Rudolph, 1990). This lack of faith was evident at The College of William and Mary, where, although the College's charter directed that faculty were to be given the authority to "appoint presidents and legislate for the college," it wasn't until thirty years after the founding of William and Mary that the college's trustees felt they could relinquish this control to the faculty members (Brubacher and Rudy, 1997, p. 26).

Faculty dissatisfaction with this model of governance helped to bring about its end and the evolution toward the concept of shared governance that is embraced as part of the modern American collegiate model. An important portent of this evolution—and of the conception of the American college that dominates today—occurred at Harvard in 1825. There, the faculty seized upon a general discontent with the administration and the relatively stagnate curriculum of the colonial college. Their protests earned them the right of internal control over the discipline of the students and the direction of instruction (Brubacher and Rudy, 1997). This right of internal control ripened over time to become the fruit known as academic freedom.

This notion of shared governance, including the idea that faculty have primary authority over the instruction and evaluation of their students, has so thoroughly permeated the American higher education landscape that today it is the normative means of governing a college. As an example of this mentality, institutions that seek an abrupt change to their institution's shared governance are often cast as less than legitimate or backwards. Yet, if we examine the concept of shared governance, we see that the areas over which faculty and administrators have had respective control have changed over time. These changes occurred in reaction to both internal and external factors. One might characterize these changes and their causes as Birnbaum (1988) does in his conception of the relationship between the technical and administrative cores of the college.

Birnbaum's Collegiate Model

Birnbaum's distinction of the two cores of the American college is helpful in a discussion of the changes in the governance roles of faculty and administrators within the model of the American college. The model (Figure 6.1) illustrates

Figure 6.1. The Core Units of the American College

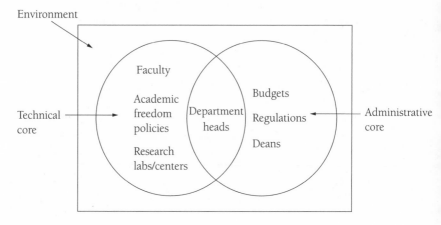

Note: Adapted from Birnbaum (1988).

what shared governance means for the American college: there are singular as well as shared areas of responsibility for both the administrative and technical elements of the college. Moreover, the construction of the model helps us to acknowledge its fluidity.

Highlighted within the model are the singular and dualistic roles played by some members of the institutions as they attempt to straddle the administrative and technical cores. The department head, for example, is an individual who, because of his administrative role and likely scholarly background, must straddle the two cores of the organization and serve as a conduit for faculty–administrative relations. The model also illustrates the traditional lack of hierarchy that is found in colleges and universities. In Birnbaum's model, each system and its actors (that is, faculty and administrators) are responsible for different elements of the college; as a result, they coexist on a horizontal, rather than vertical, plane. This collegial structure provides for the shared authority for the areas of the institution that require both academic and administrative expertise. The AAUP's argument that interdependence is a hallmark of the post-secondary institution is reflected in the interlocking nature of the technical and administrative cores.

Finally, while Figure 6.1 seems to present well-defined roles for professionals working with the college, both faculty and administrators may move between the technical and administrative cores. For example, faculty may serve on department, college, or university committees that serve administrative functions. Deans, provosts, and even presidents may choose to retain limited teaching responsibilities and, as a result, participate in the technical core of the college in that capacity.

Birnbaum's model of the American college "suggests that at least two things must be considered in designing an effective administration—the environment and the technical [cores]" (Birnbaum, 1988, p. 42). That is, the model's illustration of shared and specialized areas of authority suggests that, if the technical core of the college undergoes significant changes, the administrative core must be reorganized to address these changes in this interlocking system; this is the product of the cores' interdependence. Simultaneously, because the environment in which the college operates supplies inputs and receives outputs from the college, changes in this organizational element must also be taken into consideration by the administrative core. Birnbaum argues that these two elements (that is, the technical core and environment) are key to understanding and evaluating the administration of any college or university. This is a classically rational argument. If true, it would mean that the means by which the college or university creates and transmits knowledge (that is, the technical core) is key to understanding how the organization should be organized and governed (Pfeffer and Salancik, 1978; Meyer and Rowan, 1977). Environmental changes also impact on an organization's inputs and outputs and, as a result, on its administrative structures (Tolbert, 1985). Birnbaum (1988) argues that the effective college administrator must perceive and react to changes in her or his organization's technical core and external environment in order to maintain an effective administrative core and organization.

If this dualistic model is accurate, we might expect to see changes in the responsibilities of both the administrative and technical cores of colleges and universities. These changes would be the result of environmental changes or changes in the ways in which teaching and research (that is, the technology of the college) were conducted. Such changes would have an impact upon the interdependence of and relationship between the administrative and technical cores. In an attempt to flesh out such changes, the following sections will discuss how the relationship between the administrative and technical cores of the American college may have changed in response to changes in the technical cores and environments of these organizations. Such changes will directly affect the reality of shared governance and, as a result, our conception of how colleges can—ideally—be organized and governed.

Technical System Changes and Shared Governance

What kinds of changes in the technical core of higher education currently threaten our notion of shared governance? There are several cogent examples from recently publicized events that can be used to portray how Birnbaum's model works. First, consider changes in the ways in which knowledge is created and transmitted in today's colleges. Today, it is not unusual for students and professors to use personal and networked computers as a tool for teaching and research. Students are often given assignments that require them to use high-tech tools or on-line search engines on the Internet. These new technologies require fresh aptitudes of students, but provide a means of learning that was unavailable to past generations of students. Similarly, professors now have nearly instantaneous access to information from around the world, including large data sets and the computer hardware and statistical software that allow them to manage and analyze these data sets on their office computers.

These changes in the ways in which knowledge is available to students and professors have already altered the relationship between the technical and administrative cores. Evidence to support this claim is available in news articles describing institutional and state attempts to police the use of this technology. A recent Virginia policy—which has since been struck down by a federal court—would have prevented faculty at public institutions from accessing explicit materials without the consent of their administrative supervisor, effectively placing that supervisor in a position to approve or deny the faculty member's research (Young, 1997). These kinds of policies restrict the academic freedom of faculty members in a manner that could not have been predicted until recently. In the process, the breadth of the administrative core is increased. Where the traditional notion of shared governance placed a faculty member's research squarely within the domain of that faculty member, today we see that concept threatened by changes in the availability of certain kinds of words and images.

Changes in the technology used to create and transmit knowledge have also pushed universities into cooperative relationships with hardware and software companies. Because of the relatively high costs of adding state-of-the-art technology to classrooms and labs, colleges have embraced these cooperative relationships as a means of acquiring much-needed equipment and expertise. Yet there are critics of such plans who point to the inevitable questions such partnerships raise. A proposed plan for such a partnership at California State University (CSU) was criticized by faculty members and students. While university officials at CSU considered a partnership "as a last resort" and only because the state had refused to provide financing for necessary technological upgrades, campus faculty were concerned that "the university would be pressured by the companies to offer more distance-education courses over the Internet in place of traditional classroom instruction" as a result of the partnership (Young, 1998, p. A34). Faculty and students on CSU campuses were also concerned that they were not consulted prior to the university's negotiations with the technology companies. These kinds of cooperative partnerships with companies operating outside the academic community, while financially prudent, nurture suspicions among faculty members that their authority regarding the academic "side" of the college is being threatened. As faculty are pressured to offer courses on-line and participate in the expansion of distance education, many question whether the administration has educational or economic interests in mind, or whether the academic ramifications of such plans have been considered. More importantly, perhaps, faculty wonder how their role as teachers and researchers will be changed as a result.

Environmental Changes and Shared Governance

Changes taking place in the higher education environment are also raising new questions regarding how shared governance will function in an increasingly turbulent environment. Because the environment in which higher education institutions operate has changed so dramatically so quickly, both faculty and administrators have had to adapt haphazardly, leaving many issues regarding shared governance unanswered. It is important to note that these environmental changes are likely lasting and deserving of our attention. "Many public institutions are under pressure to demonstrate fiscal restraint. In the name of 'restructuring,' their administrators have sought to make changes that used to be left up to the faculty" (Magner, 1995). Higher education institutions, especially public colleges and universities, have faced increasing criticism from trustees and legislators that they are inefficient and bloated with unnecessary units, both academic and administrative. In the face of such criticism, many institutions have embarked upon ambitious restructuring plans or have adopted strategies to identify units that are "less central" to their mission or, because of their low productivity, are unworthy of further financial support. Too often, these strategies have failed to recognize the authority that faculty have traditionally held regarding curricular matters, such as when degree programs are closed without the consultation of faculty senates (Magner, 1995). Or when, predictably, low-status degree programs that are less likely to bring in much-needed external funding are terminated as directed by strategic plans that emphasize the administrative reallocation of resources to programs "central" to the university's mission (Slaughter and Silva, 1985; Slaughter, 1994; Morphew, 1998). As a result of these program terminations and reallocation decisions, the academic and governmental equilibrium of the college community has changed. More importantly, perhaps, these actions demonstrate to the campus community that shared governance ideals may sometimes be set aside or ignored by the campus administration.

The push toward greater efficiencies has also caused many institutions to augment their faculty membership with adjuncts—faculty members who work on a part-time basis and focus primarily on teaching. In fact, while the number of full-time higher education faculty increased by 47 percent from 1970 through 1993, the same period saw a 355 percent increase in the number of adjunct faculty members: in 1970 there were 369,000 full-time and 104,000 part-time faculty members, and in 1993 there were 546,000 full-time and 370,000 part-time faculty members (National Center for Education Statistics, 1996). While it is clear that many adjunct faculty members provide high-quality instruction for their students, the impact on shared governance is much foggier and more problematic. Adjunct faculty members, because of their part-time status and the likelihood that they hold similar positions on several campuses, may be less likely to be involved in campus governance bodies. As a result, there are increased pressures on tenured and probationary faculty members to participate in groups such as the faculty senate. Some faculty members believe that full-timers must respond to the increased use of adjuncts by becoming more active in campus budget decisions, so as to make sure that faculty lines are filled by tenure-track faculty whenever possible (Leatherman, 1997). Such calls for action suggest that faculty feel left out of crucial decisions regarding teaching assignments and the use of university financial resources.

Conclusions

Shared governance is, inarguably, one of the aspects of the American college that defines this institution. This traditional style of government within the college shapes the relationship between faculty and administrators and has a significant impact upon the college's ability to withstand changes in its environment while maintaining high standards of teaching and knowledge production. Yet shared governance is not a static condition. It is fluid over time, often responding to environmental changes, changes in the tasks of the college, or a combination of both. As a result, the areas over which faculty or administrators have authority will likely change as will the complexion and nature of the college community.

Birnbaum's (1988) model of the two cores of the American college is useful for those who are interested in understanding and documenting changes in the patterns of shared governance in higher education today. The model illustrates the fluidity and interdependence of the areas of authority for faculty and administrators within the college. The model also allows for a visualization of how changes in the environment of the college or in its technical area are likely to affect the interdependence between the administrative and technical cores.

The goal of this chapter was to help readers understand how current and future changes in the ways in which colleges work will likely affect shared governance in higher education and our notion of college. The examples cited in this chapter illustrate how shared governance is correlated with what colleges do as well as the environment within which they work. Because shared governance is part of our notion of college, we should be wary of how changes in the ways in which higher education institutions are governed will influence other aspects of our notion of college. Moreover, we should attempt to understand how environmental and technical changes will affect students' learning and the ability of faculty to create new knowledge, the two primary areas of production within higher education institutions. It is likely that changes in the ways in which colleges are governed will have an impact upon these outputs as well as affecting our notion of the American college.

References

American Association of University Professors, "Statement on Government of Colleges and Universities." *Academe,* 1996, 52 (4).

Birnbaum, R. *How Colleges Work.* San Francisco: Jossey-Bass, 1988.

Brubacher, J. S., and Rudy, W. *Higher Education in Transition: A History of American Colleges and Universities.* New Brunswick, N.J.: Transaction Publishers, 1997.

Leatherman, C. "Growing Use of Part-time Professors Prompts Debate and Calls for Action." *The Chronicle of Higher Education,* October 10, 1997, p. A14.

Lucas, C. J. *American Higher Education: A History.* New York: St. Martin's Press, 1994.

Magner, D. K. "'Restructuring' Stirs Outcry at James Madison." *The Chronicle of Higher Education,* March 3, 1995, p. A15.

Meyer, J. W., and Rowan, B. "Institutionalized Organizations: Formal Structure as Myth and Ceremony." *American Journal of Sociology,* 1977, *83* (2), 340–63.

Morphew, C. C. "Goals and Rewards: Anatomy of a Program Termination." Unpublished paper, 1998.

National Center for Education Statistics. *Digest of Education Statistics.* Washington, D.C.: US Department of Education, OERI, 1996.

Pfeffer, J., and Salancik, G. *The External Control of Organizations.* New York: Harper and Row, 1978.

Rudolph, F. *The American College and University: A History.* Athens: University of Georgia Press, 1990.

Slaughter, S. "Academic Freedom at the End of the Century." In P. G. Altbach, R. O. Berdahl, and P. J. Gumport (eds.), *Higher Education in American Society.* Amherst, N.Y.: Prometheus, 1994.

Slaughter, S., and Silva, E. "Towards a Political Economy of Retrenchment: The American Public Research Universities." *The Review of Higher Education,* 1985, *8* (40), 295–318.

Tolbert, P. S. "Institutional Environments and Resource Dependence: Sources of Administrative Structure in Institutions of Higher Education." *Administrative Science Quarterly,* 1985, *30* (1), 1–13.

Young, J. R. "Proposed Technology Deal Stirs Controversy at California State." *The Chronicle of Higher Education,* December 19, 1997. A24–A25.

Young, J. R. "Judge Strikes Down Virginia Internet Law as Unconstitutional Limit on Free Speech." *The Chronicle of Higher Education,* March 2, 1998, A34.

CHRISTOPHER C. MORPHEW *is assistant professor of higher education at the University of Kansas.*

High-profile athletic programs contribute to the collegiate ideal and are used by many institutions to provide connections to their internal and external constituents.

The Collegiate Ideal and the Tools of External Relations: The Uses of High-Profile Intercollegiate Athletics

J. Douglas Toma

Colleges and universities devote substantial resources to the concurrent tasks of constructing a positive institutional identity and raising their external profile. Capturing the attention of important outside audiences—major donors and annual fund contributors; legislative appropriation committees and tax-paying citizens; prospective students and tuition-paying parents—is often difficult. Nevertheless, it is necessary if the university is to portray itself as worthy of support from these off-campus constituents.

One aspect of the university that often does garner significant notice is the on-campus spectator sports program, particularly the marquee football and men's basketball programs at large institutions. These are the teams that generate and receive so much of the attention and revenue associated with intercollegiate athletics. Spectator sports are commonly portrayed as the front door to the university; they are what many people on the outside see and what eventually gets them inside. Especially at larger institutions, these sports are entertainment spectaculars that build and fill enormous stadia and arenas, entice television networks to broadcast games to eager national audiences, and attract hundreds of national and local journalists to campus on game day.

The magnitude of these events not only contributes an aura of importance to the campus, but they are the aspect of the university that is most visible to those outside of the academic community. The marquee sports have evolved into *the* key point of reference to the university for many important audiences, an outcome that the university has fostered through its use of college sports in campus life and external relations. High-profile sports assume an often substantial role in the personal identity of individuals—particularly students—within the university community. They are also an essential part of the personal identity of a large group of external constituents who associate with the institution primarily—if not exclusively—through teams and games. The often intense institutional identification that results from engagement with spectator sports provides the university with a critical tool in garnering support. At schools with high-profile teams, administrators involved in external relations—admissions, advancement, alumni relations, community affairs, development, governmental relations—orchestrate through college sports the involvement in campus life of key constituents that is so important in advancing various institutional ends.

My baseline contention is that college sports are significant in defining the essence of the American college and university. Higher education in the United States has never been just about the classroom or laboratory, but has embodied a romanticized collegiate ideal where academic endeavors coexist with the pursuit of campus community through customs and rituals, events and activities, and residence life and recreational facilities. Particularly at institutions with a substantial number of full-time, traditional-aged students—like most flagship state universities and large private institutions—institutional life is often as much about student activities and residence life as it is about the production and dissemination of knowledge. On larger campuses, football and basketball games serve as a surrogate for the more intimate community-building activities traditionally found on smaller residential campuses that are the basis of the collegiate ideal. Moreover, college sports have particular meaning as carriers of custom and tradition across generations and other social divides.

At the turn of the last century, although some American colleges became universities—grafting the European foci on research and graduate education onto the idea of the residential campus imported from Oxford and Cambridge—they did not adopt the European concept of a university being merely a faculty within an academic building. At the same time, financial support for American higher education remained primarily a local matter. As a result, Americans continue to relate to higher education institutions on a very personal level. Our conceptualization of the university is both as a community itself and as part of a broader community. Not only do colleges and universities assume a place of great significance in the professional lives of students, faculty, and administrators, but institutions are important in their personal lives as well. Meanwhile, there is an often intense civic engagement with institutional life. Local external constituents provide institutions with needed financial support, and institutions provide a touchstone for the surrounding community.

What results from our definition of the university as both a community itself and as part of the broader community is a pronounced affinity for institutions by both internal and external constituents. In Nebraska, for instance, citizens support the state university in Lincoln through their tax dollars, and their civic pride in that institution becomes part of who they are as Nebraskans (particularly on Saturday afternoons in the fall). As members of broadly defined university communities, both those on and off campus assume a personal and intense investment in something perceived to be significant. In short, institutions become part of our individual and collective identities.

Spectator sports provide a bridge between external constituents and the collegiate ideal. Many external constituents essentially experience the university through its football and basketball teams. Intercollegiate athletics not only entertains many of the external constituents who are so important in maintaining the university, but also involves them in institutional life in a way that is meaningful to them. If we are to understand our largest and most prominent universities, we must ask how on-campus spectator sports—particularly the high-profile sports of football and men's basketball—coincide with the identities that institutions construct for themselves and the identities that individuals derive from their institutional affiliations.

I limit my argument here to the high-profile intercollegiate athletic programs at large universities that are the exception rather than the rule across the whole of American higher education. Most participation in intercollegiate sports occurs with little fanfare. Except for the so-called revenue-producing marquee sports, varsity teams at larger schools typically receive little attention, even though they account for the bulk of participation at the varsity level. At the smaller colleges that represent most of the participation in intercollegiate sports overall, the situation parallels the typical non-revenue sport at a larger school. None of this is to say that college sports are not meaningful to campus communities at smaller schools or that non-revenue sports are not important at larger universities, particularly for the student-athletes who compete in them. The difference is in scope. At State U., football and basketball are a regional and national phenomenon, not merely a campus or local one. Small college and non-revenue college sports are rarely the window to understanding the campus that the marquee sports are at the flagship state or large private universities on which I focus.

The work of Dutton, Dukerich, and Harquail (1994) on organizational identification provides a conceptual framework for understanding this phenomenon. In their model, the strength of the positive connections that people form with organizations are a factor of (1) the attractiveness of what they perceived to be distinctive, central, and enduring about the organization; and (2) the degree to which they believe others view the organization favorably. Perceived organizational identity and construed external image are positively influenced by the level of contact that one has with the organization and the visibility of one's organizational affiliation (Mael and Tetrick, 1993; Sutton and Harrison, 1993; Dutton and Dukerich, 1991).

In a study of eleven campuses that are representative of the different types of universities that make a substantial institutional investment in intercollegiate athletics, I found that a high-profile college sports program is perceived by external constituents to be something distinctive, central, and enduring about the institution, as well as something that is viewed favorably by others. Both outcomes enhance institutional identification, causing people both to be drawn to campus and to come to know something about the institution, often something positive. These factors represent the collegiate ideal serving the goals of institutional advancement by increasing the level of contact that external constituents have with the institution and motivating them to want to enhance the visibility of their organizational affiliation.

Drawing People to Campus

It is essential for institutions to draw external constituents to campus—both literally and figuratively—if they are going to assemble the resources necessary to survive and prosper. The difficulty is capturing the attention of the right audiences for the right purposes. One particularly effective tool for reaching these audiences is through the collegiate ideal in the form of high-profile intercollegiate athletics. Football and basketball teams garner the attention for an institution that raises its overall profile in the eyes of many relevant constituents. Intercollegiate athletics afford external audiences the opportunity to become directly involved with the institution and provide them with a concrete reason to support it—even to feel passionate about it. Given the ability of high-profile spectator sports to engage people in institutional life—supplying them with something that they can champion and with which they can identify—intercollegiate athletics assumes an important position within the overall identity of the institution as the embodiment of the collegiate ideal. On-campus spectator sports serve to connect key external constituencies with "their" university, both physically and emotionally.

The intersections between external relations, the collegiate ideal, and intercollegiate athletics become clearer using three institutional functions involving external relations as illustrations: governmental relations, development, and alumni relations. Administrators who work in these areas recognize how important football and basketball games—the essence of the collegiate ideal at many large universities—are in drawing people to campus.

At public universities, intercollegiate athletics offer a useful tool in state and governmental relations. Each year, the football game between Michigan State and Michigan offers an opportunity for the administrations at both schools to invite legislators and bureaucrats from the state capital in Lansing to campus (the game is played in alternate years at each school). Once the legislators are on-campus, the universities focus on the messages that they have individually, and in conjunction with each other, identified as central. These are the ideas that they hope will soon translate into buildings and programs with the requisite state support. At Louisiana State, located only a few miles from Huey Long's state capital tower in Baton Rouge, staff from state agencies responsible for appropriations to the university are regularly invited to see football games from one of several enclosed boxes located adjacent to the press box. The games are another work day for university officers, who use the occasion to build relationships with the bureaucrats and drive home the appropriate messages about university initiatives and needs. State legislators also make use of the access provided by the university through Tiger football game tickets, dispensing them to supporters and constituents.

Similarly, campus sporting events augment university fundraising. Like other administrators, development officers are working on game days, building relationships with the potential donors that they are able to attract to campus with the promise of viewing the game from a box while enjoying catered food. Placed strategically in the box are major officers of the university poised to discuss key fundraising and resource needs when the right opportunity presents itself. At the University of Nevada at Las Vegas, certain prospective donors are invited aboard airplanes chartered to take teams to away games. Development officers also use away games as an opportunity to mobilize potential donors in those areas, inviting them to games and events surrounding them. The recent Northwestern participation in the Rose Bowl coincided with a blitz of development activity in Southern California.

Alumni associations, where fundraising typically involves more people giving less money, also typically adopt a high profile at football and basketball games. In fact, at some schools, it is difficult to find a well-attended alumni event that is not somehow connected with athletics. The hospitality tents pitched in parking lots outside of football stadiums provide the contact with alumni that is critical to enhancing alumni participation in the life of the university.

It is essential for institutions to draw external constituents to campus—both literally and figuratively—if they are going to assemble the resources necessary to survive and prosper. Drawing these people *to* campus makes it more likely that they will be drawn *into* campus, making an eventual successful "ask" (whether for state appropriations, major gifts, or annual fund contribution) more likely. Attracting important external constituents to the events surrounding games in the high-profile spectator sports that are the essence of the collegiate ideal is a key tool—perhaps *the* key tool at large institutions—available to university administrators seeking to build relationships with these groups. Even less direct engagement in campus life can yield similarly positive results for the university. Simply following teams and games from afar draws external constituents into university life in a way that enhances institutional identification and facilitates support.

Positive Perceptions of the Institution

Spectator sports events not only attract the attention and participation of key external constituents in institutional life; they also help to allow them to come to consider the university in positive terms. The interests of university faculty and administrators often coincide with enhancing the reputation and profile of the institution. As in business, a positive identity of which people are aware is the pipeline through which resources flow. The basic assumption is that neither legislative appropriation committees, nor tuition-paying parents, nor annual and major donors, will want to contribute to an enterprise that is perceived to lack significance. Accordingly, the paramount goal for any university administration is to use the tools available to improve the perception of the institution.

The key external constituencies to whom colleges and universities attempt to spread coherent and positive messages outlining institutional missions and initiatives are sometimes skeptical. Universities operate under norms that are often peculiar to people outside of academe and are not especially accessible to lay audiences. Moreover, specific programs—research in the humanities, for instance—that are at the essence of the university can be controversial and are sometimes difficult to explain to external constituencies.

Intercollegiate athletics offers the institutional advancement community the opportunity to use goodwill generated from something that is institution-wide to sell specific programs and initiatives to the key external constituents who must back them financially. On-campus spectator sports are apparent and accessible—and typically popular. Football and basketball teams and games allow advancement officers to portray an often otherwise impersonal—and sometimes even unpopular—university with a human face. Spectator sports connect external constituents to "their" institution and provide them with a feeling of (often) intense pride about it.

Of the many illustrations of the role of high-profile spectator sports in enhancing institutional identity, one of the most interesting is the role of sports in admissions—certainly for undergraduates and perhaps even for graduate and professional students—in bringing institutions to the attention of prospective students. The appeal to prospective students is the collegiate ideal. They are not drawn to an institution by the prospect of participating as student-athletes—a recruiting device used commonly and successfully at many smaller institutions—but by the opportunity of membership within a larger community of loyal fans. In other words, through an appeal to the collegiate ideal. Institutions use spectator sports in defining the institution relative to others for prospective students.

College sports is part of what makes a large state university unique and attractive to those enrolling. Mass sporting events also make the large, seemingly impersonal university seem more accessible to potential students. One-third of the photographs in the poster-size viewbook produced for prospective students by the University of Michigan in the past three years involve people watching intercollegiate athletics in some way. Admissions officers at Louisiana State University and Northwestern University reported that applications for undergraduate admissions increased by roughly one-quarter in the year following dramatic positive turnabouts in football. At Northwestern, prospective students from across the country were bombarded with stories in both the sports and regular media that portrayed the school in the most positive way. Northwestern became the model of blending academic rigor, athletic success, and good citizenship, and that has translated into more interest in the school.

Most prospective students are likely to know something positive about the university outside of intercollegiate athletics. However, high-profile spectator sports may be the only point of reference to the large university for many residents of local communities, taxpayers in a state, and people in the nation-at-large. For example, what do most people across the nation know about the University of Michigan? Perhaps only that the school has enjoyed some success in football and basketball. Most have little idea about the high ranking of most academic departments on the campus. The kids that we see at the airport in Kansas City or the shopping mall in San Diego wearing the maize and blue hats and jackets—claiming Michigan as part of their own identity—likely know little about the flagship state university beyond the famous winged helmets and the first bars of "The Victors." What they do know about is the collegiate sports aspect of Michigan, and their hats and jackets do much to raise the national profile of the institution. What is perhaps more interesting is that even in the state of Michigan, citizens may know little more. Similarly, how many people across the country (at least those outside of academe) would have even heard of Duke or Clemson or Tulane were it not for college sports? How many would ever hear anything about the states of Alabama or Nebraska or Utah were it not for the success of the football and basketball teams at their state universities? In contrast, how many people outside academe, even in Chicago, know anything about the University of Chicago, an institution that no longer participates in high-profile intercollegiate sports?

Even for those with simply a passing interest in sports, teams participating in intercollegiate football and basketball at the highest levels become household names. It would be difficult for *any* Nebraskan—or even most Americans—not to know something about the recent national champion Cornhusker football team. The team simply receives too much attention in too many places to go unnoticed. Even the person in Omaha who is indifferent to sports probably knows something about the Nebraska team, given the profile of the team in the state. If the non-sports fan does not hear about the Cornhuskers through the sports page or a sportscast, he or she will probably hear about them by reading the front page, by viewing the regular newscast, in any number of social settings, or even at the office. With that kind of pervasive notice, how could the team not become a significant aspect of the identity of the university? The point is underscored by the fact that the academic sides of so many of our large state and private universities look alike to many people, while different college football and basketball teams have unique identities. The academic programs at the University of Nebraska, Clemson University, and the University of Connecticut are very similar; however, the Cornhuskers, Tigers, and Huskies are distinctive.

Whether or not one supports the idea of high-profile intercollegiate athletics, it is difficult to deny that college sports matter greatly in the public life of the university. Football and basketball are a significant component of the overall identity of schools that invest heavily in these activities. Perhaps those constituents outside of the traditional university community are less significant in the life of the institution than are those on-campus who contribute to the life of the university more directly. Still, these are the taxpayers to whom public universities must appeal, however indirectly, for support. They are the prospective students or their parents. They are even the potential donors, both major and minor. Consequently, universities quickly recognize the value of imparting their messages externally and come to value the tools that allow for these messages to be heard. The bottom line is that managing institutional identity—however difficult that may be—becomes increasingly important in a climate of ever-increasing competition for static resources, and athletics offers a rare tool to enhance profile.

Concluding Thoughts

It is difficult to deny that sports—not just college sports, but all sports—are important in society. Because so many people are paying attention, intercollegiate athletics has become an especially important institutional function when schools make a heavy investment in sports. Athletics is a part of the university, however, that has seemingly very little to do with its fundamental purposes. How does football or basketball, when played at the highest level, contribute to research, teaching, and service—the reasons that society supports universities? How does anything associated with the collegiate side of institutional life connect with the academic side of the university that must be its core. This potentially dangerous disconnect alone offers reason to study the connections between athletics, collegiate life, and identity at our large universities.

Spectator sports—like all things collegiate on campus—are an image-building tool that must be used cautiously. If all that people know about a university is its teams, then the institution is relying upon something that is by definition inconsistent with its purposes for existence. Therefore, in order to receive the consistent support for which it hopes, it is critical that a university make the appropriate connections between athletics and academics. It is not only the right thing to do, but it is a necessary thing to do. Athletics may get an institution in the door—like the door-to-door salesperson—but unless there is something else to sell, the university will go away a failure. No university wants to be known as the type of "football factory" that sacrifices academic integrity for success on the playing field. Those at schools that have had serious problems in their football or basketball programs report that scandals in the athletic department do not necessarily undo strides made in bolstering academic reputation. However, they do suggest that these difficulties represent a serious distraction from the business of building the other aspects of the university. These troubles can also damage the community building that is the other basic intra-institutional use for high-profile intercollegiate athletics.

Given the importance college sports assumes in both community-building and raising the university profile, the potential exists for the messenger itself to become part of the overall message, and perhaps even to overpower it. It can be a tricky proposition to rely upon intercollegiate athletics to tell the story of an institution devoted to activities in classrooms and in laboratories that are far removed from the playing field. For many in society—including those on whose support public higher education relies—State U. may primarily embody a team.

These same people are likely to have some sense that State U. is a "good school," but that message rarely comes across as often and clearly as the "good place" identity fostered through spectator sports. Institutions run the same risks in using college sports in building campus community. The messenger and the message may be sufficiently intertwined that the messenger becomes the message, and that is when the scandals so often associated with an imbalance between athletics and academics arise.

The importance we often attach to intercollegiate athletics underscores the limited control that colleges and universities have over the way people receive the messages that they attempt to relate. That means that shaping or reshaping identity is a difficult proposition, even under the best circumstances. The administration at the University of Nebraska may want to talk about the exciting applied research being done in the agricultural engineering department that makes it relevant, or about its achievements in minority student recruiting that make it progressive. But many more people are much more interested in Cornhusker football than in these other programs and activities. Similarly, these same messages are often equally difficult to project to groups on campus, as those who attempt organizational change will attest. The best for which most institutions can hope is that people somehow receive their message—even if it is during the "this is State U." commercial included during half-time of televised games—and they integrate enough of it to equate the institution with something of value.

Another explanation for the disconnect between athletics and academe may lie in the traditional rationales offered for intercollegiate athletics versus the reality of college sports on our campuses. Long-standing justifications for high-profile college sports include making much-needed money for the university and building character among student-athletes. These stated rationales ring hollow, particularly today. Only a small handful of the schools that support high-profile athletics programs are making more than they contribute in state money or student fees. Similarly, the character-building argument may apply to non-revenue or small college intercollegiate sports, but it has little to do with high-profile football and basketball programs at our largest universities. The scandals that seem to dog many of these programs represent but one example of the consequences of the disconnect between athletics and academe. Clearly, the moral victories associated with effort, self-improvement, and sportsmanship that may mark some small college and non-revenue sports have little meaning within the high-stakes worlds of high-profile intercollegiate football and basketball.

Intercollegiate athletics serves an important purpose within the university, both in fostering the on-campus community associated with collegiate life, and in providing a vehicle for advancing institutional goals with important off-campus constituents. College sports are a significant, but overlooked, aspect of the American university. If we are to understand the places that invest in high-profile athletics programs—our largest and most important universities—we must appreciate the ways in which intercollegiate athletics coincide with the identities that campuses define for themselves. The utility of athletics in advancing institutional ambitions is undeniable, but there are potential dangers involved when universities define their identities around a construct that is often so far removed from the academic activities rightly at the center of our higher education institutions.

References

Dutton, J. E., and Dukerich, J. M. "Keeping an Eye on the Mirror: Image and Identity in Organizational Adaptation." *Academy of Management Journal,* 1991, *34,* 517–554.

Dutton, J. E., Dukerich, J. M., and Harquail, C. V. "Organizational Images and Member Identification." *Administrative Science Quarterly,* 1994, *39,* 239–263.

Mael, F. A., and Tetrick, L. E. "Identifying Organizational Identification." *Educational and Psychological Measurement,* 1993, *52* (4), 813–824.

Sutton, C. D., and Harrison, A.W. "Validity Assessment of Compliance, Identification, and Internalization as Dimensions of Organizational Commitment." *Educational and Psychological Measurement,* 1993, *53* (1), 217–224.

J. DOUGLAS TOMA is assistant professor of higher education at the University of Missouri-Kansas City and visiting assistant professor and senior research fellow at the Graduate School of Education and Institute for Research on Higher Education at the University of Pennsylvania.

Although fiscal restraints have impacted all levels of postsecondary education, community college vocational programs have been particularly hard hit. This chapter presents a thorough examination of present conditions, challenges the vision of "place," and provides a realistic approach toward the "ideal" within vocational education community college programs.

Vocational Education and the Collegiate Ideal: The Threat and the Challenge of Limited Resources

Linda Serra Hagedorn

Community colleges do not fit the traditional definition of the collegiate ideal. Devoid of residence halls, dining facilities, strict admissions criteria, Greek organizations, active alumni groups, and other trappings associated with the "ivory tower" myth, typical community colleges must function in urban environments and provide educational services to large numbers of part-time students who juxtapose family, job, and college. Although concepts of ideal and place are applicable within the community college environment, the terms are elusive and in dire need of redefinition. But perhaps the community college programs presenting the biggest challenge to traditional definitions of collegiate ideal and the concept of place are those in vocational (non-transfer) subjects. Further complicating and challenging the ideal is the widespread phenomenon of declining resources. Although the challenge of effectively apportioning dwindling funds while still maintaining (or even improving) productivity exists for all college types and programs, the problem is especially acute in the fastest growing segment of higher education—namely community college vocational programs (Grubb, 1995). The present chapter describes the effects of limited and declining resources on the collegiate ideal as framed within the vocational education environment of public community colleges. After a description of vocational education and postsecondary vocational students, I discuss the fiscal realities and associated challenges with respect to this segment of education. I then describe and elaborate on the role of contract education in counterbalancing fiscal and other problems specifically pertinent to vocational education. I conclude with observations regarding superoptimum solutions and a second look at the collegiate ideal. To assist in the definition of the ideal within the parameters of a nontraditional environment, I queried and observed faculty, students, and administrators in vocational community college programs.

Vocational Education, Ideal, and Place

The term "vocational program" is broadly defined by the federal Carl D. Perkins Vocational and Applied Technology Education Act of 1990[1] as "organized educational programs offering a sequence of courses which are directly related to the preparation of individuals in paid or unpaid employment in current or emerging occupations requiring other than a baccalaureate or advanced degree" (Public Law 101-392). The Perkins Act provides secondary and postsecondary institutions with approximately $1.6 billion dollars for use in vocational programs.[2] Vocational programs in community colleges are instrumental in providing training to the workforce of the future (American Association of Community Colleges, 1998). The majority of the approximately 4.3 million students enrolled in vocational education (43 percent of all undergraduate students) are earning their credits at public community colleges (U.S. Department of Education, 1989). In fact, since 78 percent of enrollments in institutions offering less than the baccalaureate are in vocational subjects, the principal educational mission of most community colleges is vocational training (U.S. Department of Education, 1989). Vocational programs attract a diverse student pool of recent high school graduates, workforce participants seeking to update work skills, hobbyists and retired individuals pursuing personal interests, and postsecondary degree holders (of all levels) seeking "practical" education, usually for career reasons. Vocational students are more likely than their peers in transfer programs to be "nontraditional" (that is, from lower socioeconomic brackets, racial or ethnic minorities, older, or enrolled part time) (U.S. Department of Education, 1989). According to the American Association of Community Colleges (1998), each year more than 450,000 associate degrees and approximately 200,000 certificates are granted by U.S. community colleges. However, despite the large number of vocational certificates and degrees, completion rates for post-secondary vocational students, especially among minorities and the handicapped, is low and declining (U.S. Department of Education, 1989).

In the midst of definitions of vocational education and the community college student, the concept of collegiate ideal requires a new conceptualization. Rather than being in search of bucolic pastures where academic pursuits reign supreme, vocational students seek a "place" more analogous to the *workplace* where training and skills replace scholarly inquiry. Here the collegiate ideal defines the faculty as mirrors of supervisors and managers, and academic pursuits require practicality. Although vocational students may appreciate and frequent the college library, the concept of "books as tools to learning" is expanded to include manuals, electrical components, hardware, tools, and technology. Finally, the paternalism characterized by Rudolph as the "agency that perhaps best served the purposes of the collegiate way" (1990, p. 103) is also in need of scrutiny. Paternalism extends through mentors, role models, and others who participate in the training of the "whole person." In vocational education instructing the "whole person" includes instruction in business etiquette, work ethics, punctuality, responsibility, and other peripheral traits that are necessary for career success. Therefore, a form of a collegiate ideal exists in vocational education, but it differs from that of the more traditional college program. The biggest threat to the ideal, however, is fiscal restraint.

The Fiscal Reality in Postsecondary Vocational Education

The reality of fiscal restraint is probably the greatest threat to the collegiate ideal as defined by vocational education. This situation is probably exacerbated by predictions of increasing numbers of people pursuing all types of higher education. Further, the costs of providing education are predicted to increase more rapidly than inflation. Thus, it will be necessary to "spend increasing amounts per student for increasing numbers of students just to keep pace with current trends" (Carroll and Bryton, 1997, p. 2). As with all sectors of public education, the finance and governance structure of community colleges is mainly state-based. Each state devises its allocation formulas for Perkins federal funds specifically tailored to its vocational programs as well as to its general or overall funding formulas. Unfortunately, the amounts available for allocation funding and competitive grants under the Carl D. Perkins Vocational and Applied Technology Act have recently been decreased due to reduced Congressional appropriations.

The sharing of state allocations with the Department of Corrections and health care further complicates the community college funding situation because both of these state-supported services have established a pattern of ever-increasing needs. For example, in the state of California the proportion of general funds to be allocated to community colleges in fiscal year 2005 will be identical to the proportion allocated in fiscal year 1995, namely 3 percent (Carroll and Bryton, 1997). But, while the corrections system in California was allocated 9 percent of the state's general funds in fiscal year 1995, the allocation will increase to 20 percent in the year 2005. Likewise, health care in California continues to demand larger and larger proportions of state funding. As state funds dwindle, colleges have generally responded with increases in tuition (Gates and Stone, 1997).

But experience has revealed that increased tuition only leads to the need for more substantial aid packages to support access to low income students. What have community colleges done to counteract declining allocations and increasing student pools? The state of California answered declining revenues by directing the community college system to cut costs by $10 million annually for the next four years. California is similar to other states forced to enact "quality-insensitive cost cutting" and thereby driven to increased reliance on the private sector in the form of grants, gifts, donations, partnerships with businesses, and endowments (Carroll and Bryton, 1997, p. 3). Many community college systems also look to technology and advances in distance education as possible redeemers from constrained resource catastrophes. Although a threat to more traditional definitions of "place," technology is a major partner in revised contemporary definitions of the collegiate ideal for all sectors of postsecondary education.

Though fiscal concerns exist in all disciplines and departments, fiscal restraint adversely and disproportionately impacts vocational education. The underlying cause is the explosive growth of technology. Technological advances must be employed and followed in vocational classrooms more promptly and in greater proportion than in typical liberal arts (transfer) courses. For instance, although the teaching and content of history, political science, and English have changed during recent years, the bulk of the changes are manifest in textbook revisions, teaching methodology changes, and similar relatively low-cost changes. On the other hand, modern advances have changed auto, diesel, and aero technologies to the extent that equipment purchased even five years ago is completely useless. For example, a recent community college visit and interview with the instructor of aeronautics maintenance technology revealed that recent changes in airframe and power plant mechanics made older training facilities and programs completely obsolete. This community college recently completed a state-of-the-art training facility costing over $7.5 million. In the words of the center's director; "We had to update. We were turning out obsolete workers and the employers just weren't hiring them. It was a matter of survival" (interview with the author, 1998). Similarly, a graphic arts instructor at another community college expressed her feelings:

> In graphic arts, you cannot attract students without the proper and up-to-date technology. You must train students on the same technological level that will be expected of them in industry. If you aren't training students for the workplace, then their education is a waste [interview with the author, 1998].

It is abundantly clear that as technology evolves it necessitates changes in manufacturing and equipment servicing such that vocational programs must upgrade and replace equipment, develop new and more appropriate courses, and alter instructional methods to properly train the future workforce. Thus, in redefining "the ideal" in the vocational environment the vision of "a place" is pushed aside and replaced with the need to make the college a better mirror of the "workplace."

Realistically Speaking. It is very expensive to provide cutting-edge training to vocational students. Increasingly departments have been forced to rely on external funding sources, gifts, and donations. For example, the aeronautics maintenance department of a western community college has become reliant on the periodic donations of aircraft components and technical publications. A computer information systems (CIS) department of a community college on the west coast relies on the donations of software by textbook publishing companies in exchange for adoption of their textbooks. Yet another example is the electronics technology program of a community college in the Midwest that relies on industry to donate electronic components and spare materials for student use. Each of these scenarios is an example of trading educational autonomy for necessary supplies. The electronics technology department does not necessarily receive needed components or those in short supply, but only the overflow of whatever happens to be in excess or no longer needed by the benefactor. Thus, class projects are planned to harmonize with donations rather than freely flowing from pedagogical insight. In terms of the traditional collegiate ideal, scholarly pursuits are constrained by practical availability.

State and local appropriations provide about 65 percent of the total revenues for community college vocational training (U.S. Department of Education, 1989). Donations make up a minuscule portion of the shortfall between governmental support and adequate financial resources. The bulk of the deficit between funding and the cost of vocational programs is increasingly supplied through external grants. In fact, support from the private sector has roughly doubled in the past twenty years (Carroll and Bryton, 1997). The need for and reliance on outside funding is reflected in the emergence of grants offices in most community colleges. The vice-president in charge of vocational education of a large community college explained the situation: "Outside funding is very important. Funding sources drive many of our programs. We have a grants office that is very willing to help and encourage faculty to write for money" (interview with the author, 1998).

But what happens when programs must rely on sources? Can faculty be expected to be experts at the grant writing process? A recent interview with the department chair of the engineering and technology department of a large urban community college explained:

> I just have too much work to apply for grants. I teach 24 hours a week, prepare lessons, work with students, grade assignments, plus administrative duties. My department suffers because we just can't find the time [interview with the author, 1998].

The graphic arts instructor, who recently upgraded and redesigned a computer arts laboratory through a large National Science Foundation grant combined with several smaller grants, also lamented the present situation.

> I think of myself as an entrepreneur. I used to do research, curriculum development, and teaching, but now I find my time increasingly taken up by fund raising. I have no choice; without the external grants we would be up the creek [interview with the author, 1998].

All of the community college professionals interviewed[3] agreed that present funding allocations force extensive reliance on grants for new equipment, updates, and maintenance. If seed money to begin a program is secured, there is no guarantee that monies will be available to continue the program. Furthermore, it is even more difficult to fund maintenance and to upgrade equipment. As one instructor explained, continuance funds lack the appeal and glamour of starting a program (interview with the author, 1998).

Although the reliance on grants adds additional strains to definitions of collegiate ideal and place, such grants are a necessity in these times of fiscal restraint. Since grants are scarce for vocational programs, insightful administrators and instructors have resorted to other tactics to bring money into needy vocational training departments—namely contract education.

The New Market—Contract Education

Although contract education is not a new concept in community colleges, the extensive use of and reliance on contracts and partnerships to meet community college needs is a relatively new phenomenon. Many colleges now provide (and advertise for) customized services for local businesses and industry. Public colleges have emerged into the competitive marketplace providing tailored services, alternative approaches, and client-driven educational services, frequently at the client's site and at no cost to the taxpayer. Realizing financial as well as other potential benefits of these partnerships, colleges have developed whole new departments, hired astute administrators, recruited full- and part-time instructors with recent industry experience, and developed elegant brochures and information packets to attract local business and industry. The benefits extend beyond the financial as these programs involve students in the very industries in which they are employed and occur within the "place" where their skills will be applied. Contracts with local industries seamlessly blend "out-of-classroom experiences" with those more directly related to the classroom.

In truth, contract education creates a situation as far from the traditional definition of "collegiate ideal" as imaginable. By no stretch of the imagination can one equate the experiences of students involved in contract education with those of traditional residential college students. No matter how it is bent, creased, examined, or turned, vocational college students do not fit the traditional mold. Consequently, rather than trying to create a vision of the "collegiate ideal" that creates an illusion of fit, a new "ideal," attainable, possible, and mindful of financial restraints, seems a more reasonable alternative for these students. For example, instead of high value on scholarly classics, the ideal for vocational education places emphasis and importance on keeping up with the latest technological advances. Partnerships can function as a bridge for community college faculty to experience and learn what technological advances have been implemented locally and what current and prospective employees are expected to know and perform. As equipment is upgraded, the contract education modules will be updated, narrowing the typical gap between industry standard and curriculum content. Although contract education is not a panacea for community college programs, it can be instrumental in helping fiscally constrained departments present quality instruction in appropriate environments. Rather than the optimal conclusion, contract education may better be termed a "superoptimum solution."

The Collegiate Ideal or Superoptimum Solution?

As repeatedly demonstrated throughout this chapter, "the ideal" as traditionally conceived is not a viable target in vocational community college education. Therefore, rather than aiming at an impossible target, it would appear more sensible to work toward alternative approaches. I present the superoptimum solution as a possible answer to the morass of trying to fit vocational programs within traditional definitions of the "collegiate ideal." According to Nagel and Mills (1992), a superoptimum solution is "objectively better than what has traditionally been considered to be the best solution to that type of problem" (p. 281). In other words, pursuing the superoptimum may be a realistic alternative to the ephemeral ideal. For that reason, instructional contracts or partnerships between the vocational units of community colleges and local businesses will be examined through the lens of Nagel and Mills's (1992) seven ways of arriving at a superoptimum solution (see Table 8.1).

It is easy to see how business–college contracts achieve the first point of the superoptimum; expanding the resources available. Certainly the proliferation of new departments dedicated to these arrangements attests to resource expansion. The second point, setting higher goals than what was previously considered the best while still preserving realism, is also pertinent. Without partnerships, keeping vocational education synchronized with the latest technology is virtually impossible. Partnerships do and can allow programs to realistically set higher goals.

Partnerships also fulfill the third point as they provide situations where one side can receive big benefits but the other side incurs only small costs. Actually, both sides (business and the college) may reap significant benefits. But one cannot ignore the costs incurred by the college. It appears that the

Table 8.1. Nagel and Mill's Seven Ways of Arriving at a Superoptimum Solution

1. Expand available resources.
2. Set goals higher than what was previously considered the best, while preserving realism.
3. Orchestrate outcomes so that one side receives big benefits while the other side incurs only small costs.
4. Involving a third party benefactor, which is usually a government agency.
5. Combine alternatives that are not mutually exclusive.
6. Remove or decrease sources of conflict between liberals and conservatives, rather than trying to synthesize their separate proposals.
7. Develop a package of alternatives that would satisfy both liberal and conservative goals.

Source: Nagel and Mills, 1992, pp. 281–282.

largest cost or liability is the loss of independence, autonomy, or curricular freedom. Partnerships may prevent administrators or faculty from significantly departing from curriculums or courses that do not benefit the partnership.

Although these losses cannot be labeled trivial, they may survive the Kaldor Criterion. The Kaldor Criterion is frequently used as an aid to guide public policy decisions based on benefits and losses. A policy fulfills the Criterion when those who benefit can compensate those who might lose, especially if the gainers compensate the losers (Miller, 1992). In terms of educational partnerships, the gainers are industries who can compensate the college through use of equipment, facilities, and the hiring of program graduates.

The fourth point of the superoptimum (third party benefactor) may best be understood through the following external example. While the Medicare program provides free health care to the elderly (an obvious benefit), doctors and hospitals also benefit through large volumes of medical services for and hospital stays by this segment of the population. The significant funds from treating the elderly would not accrue if the elderly purchased only the affordable amount of health care. In like fashion, partnerships provide benefits to the college by providing additional revenue streams, but also provide an affordable and available means of education to local businesses and industries.

In relation to the fifth point of the superoptimum, partnerships combine alternatives that are not mutually exclusive: education funded by both the public and the private sectors. In truth, all public postsecondary education is funded by a combination of public and private funds. Public colleges and universities are increasingly dependent on funds from student tuition, alumni gifts, grants from private foundations, and other non-governmental sources. Partnerships therefore amplify the extent of non-governmental funding at a time when governmental appropriation is diminished.

Another way of interpreting the sixth way of the superoptimum is to achieve a viable alternative such that both parties to a conflict are satisfied. In the present scenario, the parties to the conflict can be portrayed as those favoring benefits to private interests versus proponents of the public good (here, education). As illustrated, industry–college partnerships have the potential to provide benefits to both sides.

Finally, the last way to Nagel and Mill's superoptimum may be most perplexing of all: develop a package of alternatives that satisfies the goals of both sides. Astute administrators and financial officers of community colleges experiencing financial strains must be careful not to enter into contracts prior to exploring the full extent of impacts to the college. Figure 8.1 is provided as an aid in viewing the benefits and liabilities of contract education with respect to productivity, efficiency, and excellence of the college. The left side of the figure is based on Epstein's (1992) four basic ways to produce an efficient and effective outcome while the right side of the figure is based on Ruppert's (1994) five objectives of higher education systems. Examining costs and benefits from both sides of the figure may help inform a decision as to the suitability of contract education.

Figure 8.1. A Decision-Making Conceptual Framework

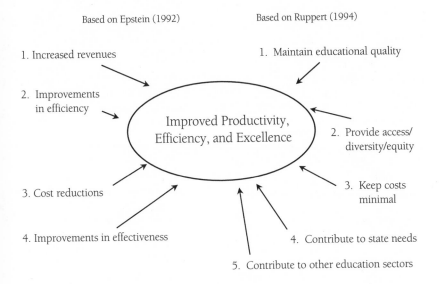

Based on Epstein (1992)   Based on Ruppert (1994)

1. Increased revenues   1. Maintain educational quality

2. Improvements
   in efficiency
                        Improved Productivity,
                        Efficiency, and Excellence   2. Provide access/
                                                              diversity/equity

3. Cost reductions   3. Keep costs
                                                            minimal

4. Improvements in effectiveness   4. Contribute to state needs

                            5. Contribute to other education sectors

Conclusions

I have argued that the traditional definition of "collegiate ideal" is inappropriate for vocational community college students. Further, I have argued for an updated and more sober definition that realistically portrays and includes typical vocational students and programs. Finally, in the redefinition, I have urged consideration and incorporation of fiscal restraints. In this realistic approach, I have offered the superoptimum as a viable target. I choose to conclude by turning my original hypothesis upside down. Rather than argue how the collegiate ideal doesn't fit, let me briefly indicate where it does fit. Despite nontraditional surroundings, students in contract educational surroundings are not left without the concept of "place." Their place is practical and seamlessly transforms learning to working. The Chickering and Kytle chapter in this volume maintains that the traditional "ideal" served two purposes: to motivate students to invest in themselves and to recognize living-learning interactions in academic life (Chickering and Kytle, 1999). Contract education has a chance of fitting this definition. The practicality of contract education motivates students to invest in their own learning and potentials. Also, contract education creates a living–learning interaction enveloped by a learning–working environment. Finally, the traditional collegiate ideal's residential origins means that students study, live, eat, and play at one location; the university becomes their way of life. Vocational community college students involved in partnerships with industry do not literally live at their workplace but spend significant amounts of time in a seamless blend of work and study that may create a superoptimum proxy for residential status.

Notes

1. The Carl D. Perkins Vocational and Applied Technology Education Act of 1990 (Public Law 101-392) is frequently referred to as VATEA.

2. The Perkins Act includes a number of "set-asides" dictating how the funds are to be used. Allocations are calculated on a state-by-state basis per a complex formula involving enrollment levels and special populations (Grubb, 1995). The set-aside provision consists of 57 percent of allocations for services to the disadvantaged, people who are handicapped, adults, single parents and homemakers, persons in nontraditional areas with respect to their sex, and the incarcerated. The rest of the funds (43 percent) are to be used for program improvement, modernization, and expansion (U.S. Department of Education, 1989).

3. A total of fifteen interviews with community college faculty (from diverse vocational areas) were conducted in three states (California, Hawaii, and Illinois) in preparation for the writing of this chapter. One administrator in charge of vocational education was also interviewed for each state.

References

American Association of Community Colleges. *Pocket Profile of Community Colleges: Trends & Statistics 1997–1998*. Washington, D.C., 1998.

Benjamin, R., and Carroll, S. *The Case for Institutional Redesign of Higher Education*. Santa Monica, Calif.: Rand Institute on Education and Training, January, 1995. (P–7939)

Carroll, S. and Bryton, E. *Higher Education's Fiscal Future*. Santa Monica, Calif.: Rand Institute on Education and Training, 1997. (DRU–1601–IET)

Chickering, A., and Kytle, J., "The Collegiate Ideal in the Twenty-First Century." In J. D. Toma and A. Kezar (eds.), *Collegiate Living, Collegiate Learning*, New Directions for Higher Education, no. 105. San Francisco: Jossey-Bass, 1999, pp. 109–120.

Epstein, P. "Measuring the Performance of Public Services." In M. Holzer (ed.), *Public Productivity Handbook*. New York: Marcel Dekker, Inc., 1992, pp. 161–194.

Gates, S., and Stone, A. *Understanding Productivity in Higher Education*. Santa Monica, Calif.: Rand Institute on Education and Training, 1997. (DRU–1596–IET)

Grubb, W. N. "The Returns to Education and Training in the Sub-baccalaureate Labor Market: Evidence from the Survey of Income and Program Participation 1984–1990." [http://ncrve.berkeley.edu/AllInOne/MDS–765.html], May, 1995.

Miller, G. J. "Cost-Benefit Analysis." In M. Holzer (ed.), *Public Productivity Handbook,* New York: Marcel Dekker, Inc., 1992, pp. 253–279.

Nagel, S. S., and Mills, M. K. "Approaches to Arriving at Superoptimum Solutions." In M. Holzer (ed.), *Public Productivity Handbook*. New York: Marcel Dekker, Inc., 1992, pp. 281–306.

Public Law 101-392, Carl D. Perkins Vocational and Applied Technology Education Act of 1990.

Rudolph, F. *The American College and University: A History*. Athens, Ga.: The University of Georgia Press, 1990.

Ruppert, S. *Charting Higher Education Accountability: A Sourcebook on State-Level Performance Indicators*. Denver, Colo.: Education Commission for the States, 1994. (ED 375 789)

U.S. Department of Education. *National Assessment of Vocational Education: Summary of Findings and Recommendations*. Final Report, Vol. I. Washington, D.C., 1989. (ED 317 659)

LINDA SERRA HAGEDORN *is assistant professor in the Center for Higher Education Policy Analysis in the School of Education at the University of Southern California. She is also program chair of the educational leadership programs emphasizing community college leadership.*

By developing community–university relationships, the urban
university expands and improves upon the idea of "place" as conceived
of in the collegiate ideal.

Redefining Campus: Urban Universities and the Idea of Place

Erin McNamara Horvat, Kathleen M. Shaw

The collegiate ideal has been synonymous with, among other things, a bucolic, pastoral environment. Removed from the hustle and bustle of everyday life, students and faculty are left to ponder the eternal truths and questions of our world, unaffected by the "real world" concerns that can muddy their thinking and distract their intellectual pursuits. Set apart both literally and figuratively, the collegiate ideal as embodied in traditional, four-year colleges and universities provides an insular environment designed to attend to the social, intellectual, and emotional needs of the student.

This persistent fixation on the self-contained pastoral model of higher education reveals a set of assumptions about both education and American society. As Riesman (1967) points out, the collegiate ideal has its roots in the uniquely American "fear of the city and its corruption" (p. 477), in which the urban landscape has the potential to contaminate both the learning process and students themselves. When combined with the premise that intellectual pursuit should be apolitical and "objective," education and the "real world"—particularly urban areas—become dichotomous concepts (Lagemann, 1993).

We believe this dichotomy to be a false one. Far from corrupting the learning process, the urban environment provides an unparalleled opportunity for an intellectual community to test its ideas against the complex reality of life as it is lived in this country's major cities. Moreover, in embracing its mission to live as part of, rather than apart from, the urban environment, the urban university provides a model for community–university relationships that expands and improves upon the idea of "place" as conceived of in the collegiate ideal.

In the pages that follow, we focus on the unique and important role that urban universities have played and continue to play in developing a concept of place that responds to the challenges of the twenty-first century. We begin by briefly reviewing the assumptions that underlie the collegiate ideal, and we delineate how they relate to the special case of the urban university and its role in our system of higher education. Then, using a case study approach, we describe several ways in which one urban university has expanded the idea of place by embracing the urban setting as an extension of the university campus. Finally, we examine the rising threats to the urban university and their implications for American society.

The Collegiate Ideal

The collegiate ideal is often held up as a model to which all other institutions, regardless of differences in mission, student body, or geographical location, should be compared. Intellectually, this ideal is most aptly described by Robert Maynard Hutchins of the University of Chicago (Lagemann, 1994, p. 124), who described the ideal university as "a haven where the search for truth may go on unhampered by utility or pressure for results." For Hutchins, the search for "truth" was directly at odds with the search for practical knowledge to be used for the public good or for service to society. This notion that the intellectual pursuit of knowledge should remain separate from the real-world concerns of society provides one of the foundations of the collegiate ideal.

The collegiate ideal is predicated on the notion that colleges and universities serve "traditional" students. While such a designation was once reserved solely for white, middle-class males, students currently defined in this manner are between the ages of eighteen and twenty-two, attend school full-time, reside on or near the college campus, and are not distracted by family or work concerns. Such conditions are crucial to sustaining the collegiate ideal, because they enable students to immerse themselves in the intellectual and social life of the college and exclude other, more mundane concerns.

Defining the Urban University

Despite the desire of many to cling to the collegiate ideal and its grounding in the agrarian past of this country, the American university has undergone several transformations during its relatively brief, though illustrious, history in this nation (Veysey, 1965). By responding to the needs of society, the university has transformed itself from a small elite training ground for the ministry to a large complex system of education serving hundreds of thousands of students annually.

These changes are due in substantial part to changes in the demographics of the country. In stark contrast to the predominantly rural population at the turn of the previous century, this country approaches the year 2000 with over 75 percent of its citizens residing in urban metropolises (U.S. Department of Commerce, Bureau of the Census, 1990). The vast majority of nonwhite populations live in urban areas, and immigrant groups, particularly Hispanic and Asian, are clustered primarily in major urban areas such as Chicago, Los Angeles, and Miami (Estrada, 1989).

While the concept of the urban university was set forth as early as 1743 in the words of Benjamin Franklin's original plan for the University of Pennsylvania (Hackney, 1993, p. 313), the term cannot be applied universally to those institutions that reside within the confines of our cities; location is only part of what distinguishes these institutions from their more traditional cousins. Rather, it is the confluence of a set of characteristics that, when taken together, define a university as "urban" in both philosophy and action. Those institutions that we define as "urban" not only serve a diverse and often disadvantaged student population that resides in the metropolitan area; they also actively embrace this mission, and seek to develop a mutually beneficial relationship with the urban setting (Adamany, 1994). More than any other type of post-secondary institution, urban universities approach the city as a great educational laboratory from which both faculty and students can learn. As Peggy Gordon Elliott states, "they are not simply in or near the city; they are of the city" (Elliott, 1994, p. 23). In short, the city is the lifeblood of the urban university.

While there is a well-documented "town–gown" tension between most institutions of higher education and their neighbors, urban universities distinguish themselves from other sectors of post-secondary education by attempting to address these tensions head-on. This stance is due in part to the mission of these institutions, but also in part to necessity. In addition to supplying an incredible diversity of students, urban areas also serve as a natural laboratory of sorts, offering unequaled opportunities for students and faculty to both contribute to and learn from an often-troubled but enormously exciting environment. In a very real sense, the boundary between the urban university and the city in which it exists is permeable. By approaching the urban environment as an extension of the campus, urban universities expand and reinvent the idea of "place." No longer does the campus end at the gates to the university. Rather, the urban university is deeply and meaningfully connected to the city in which it resides; the city constitutes its classroom, laboratory, and partner.

Temple University and the City as Classroom, Laboratory, and Partner

To provide some concrete illustrations of the ways in which urban universities interact with the broader community to redefine the idea of "place," we utilize our own institution, Temple University, as an example. Located in a poor, predominantly African-American section of the city of Philadelphia, Temple has, from its founding in 1913, been devoted to educating the poor and working-class residents of the city. These individuals have been famously referred to as the "acres of diamonds" that exist at Temple's own back door—uncut, perhaps, but with a shining core of potential that must not be squandered. In what follows, we offer three distinct yet interrelated approaches to expanding the urban university campus far past the boundaries of its formal confines.

The City as Classroom. Service learning is a pedagogical and philosophical practice that has been gaining increasing popularity at a range of colleges and universities (Rhoads, 1998); however, it is used to particularly powerful effect when offered within an urban setting. Designed to create an interplay between abstract, "book" theory and real-life application, service learning also requires students to learn within the context of providing assistance to a group of people, most often those that are without the resources to achieve their goals without that help.

Temple University offers a particularly potent example of the ways in which service learning can function at an urban university. SHINE is an acronym for Students Helping In the Naturalization of Elders. In this program, students enrolled in traditional undergraduate and graduate-level courses elect to help elderly immigrants achieve the English-language literacy they will need to become naturalized citizens of the United States. With the cooperation of faculty members teaching these courses and those who oversee SHINE, each student works on the project for a semester, and produces a major written paper that provides a systematic analysis of the experience. In particular, students are able to examine the immigrant experience and the way in which immigration policy affects the life chances of these individuals. In this way, SHINE and other service learning projects like it render the entire city of Philadelphia a classroom in which students can gain valuable insight into the challenges faced by urban residents. Moreover, students can apply this first-hand knowledge to the more traditional "book learning" of their classroom, resulting in an enriching and more meaningful educational experience.

The City as Laboratory. Perhaps because of its strong urban mission, Temple has attracted a faculty whose interests disproportionately lie in some element of the urban environment or experience. Faculty members from across the university consistently conduct research and publish books and articles that examine the urban environment from the perspective of education, social services, social policy, and history. Often, the work that is produced by these scholars is interdisciplinary in nature, reflecting the complexity of the topic itself.

For example, a team of Temple University researchers is embarking on a five-year study of an attempt to improve the quality of child care available to poor Philadelphia residents. This team consists of a policy analyst, two psychologists, a media expert, and several early childhood education specialists. Like most research conducted by university-based researchers, this project will undoubtedly result in scholarly publications for those involved. Yet the project distinguishes itself in that it will also be of direct benefit to Philadelphia residents who struggle to obtain high-quality daycare for their children, especially those who are affected by recent welfare reforms.

This urban focus has been institutionalized in some departments. The university has both a department of Geography and Urban Studies and an Urban Education program (one of only five in the country). Both approach their subject areas from an interdisciplinary perspective and have attracted faculty from sociology, public health, history, and education. However, even more "traditional" departments have formalized their interest in urban settings. In 1996 the Department of Sociology began to use metropolitan Philadelphia as the core of its graduate-level programs. In this department, students learn sociological theory, develop methodological expertise, and conduct independent research using the city as a laboratory.

Across the university, both undergraduate and graduate students benefit from the urban focus of many of the Temple University faculty. Students develop their writing skills while exploring an environment that is intimately familiar to them; they understand abstract theory through the lens of an urban setting; and they develop first-hand knowledge of the city by participating in the wide array of faculty research projects focused on the urban environment.

The City as Partner. A related yet distinct approach to expanding the boundaries of the urban education campus is the city-as-partner effort. Not quite research and distinct from pure service, this effort is an attempt to let pockets of the urban community guide the research and service activities of the university community.

The Professional Development Schools Project housed at the university's College of Education is just such an initiative. Under this seven-year-old effort, the university and a cluster of Philadelphia public schools have formed a collaboration aimed at "improving the educational climate and learning environment for (K–16) students in the city of Philadelphia through enhanced preparation of teachers and other school professionals, support for educational reform, and connection of research with practice" (Temple University, 1996). In this model, the Professional Development Schools serve as points of partnership for practitioners and researchers, enhancing both the research undertaken at the schools and the practice at those sites. However, the most potent result of this partnership might be the ability for practicing teachers to influence the research agenda of their university partners in this collaborative effort.

Challenges to the Urban University Mission

Despite the nobility of the urban university mission, many of these institutions are facing enormous pressures that threaten to alter, or perhaps destroy, the unique ways in which they have adapted to and embraced their urban settings. Again, we turn to our own university as a case in point.

Temple is currently encountering challenges from an array of fronts. Enrollment has been dropping at a rate of about 4 percent per year for the last three years; the state legislature has repeatedly decreased its financial support of the university; and the public school system from which Temple draws many of its students remains troubled. In the face of these pressures, the President recently announced that the institution will "adjust to the market" by eliminating remediation, increasing admissions standards, and developing the university's suburban campuses (*Philadelphia Inquirer,* February 9, 1998, p. A1). These policy changes are explicitly designed to attract suburban students, who are perceived to be of better "quality." In addition, the university is poised to embark on an $800 million capital improvement plan that includes the construction of three new residence halls and the development of distance learning and online computer courses (O'Neill, 1998).

In many ways, these changes could be interpreted as Temple's attempt to become a more "traditional" university, with a higher proportion of middle-class, residential students. As such, it may be moving closer to the "collegiate ideal," and within a decade, the type of education that it provides may be indistinguishable from that offered at many fine research universities across the country. But will such an education necessarily be an improvement? As we approach the next century, the gap between the "haves" and the "have-nots" continues to widen. The wealthy and well-educated erect real and symbolic gated communities with which to keep the rest of the world at bay. This trend can only result in catastrophe if permitted to continue.

Yet the permeable boundaries that exist between urban universities and their environment are an antidote to this trend. By maintaining their commitment to educating urban populations and by building on and contributing to the urban landscape, these institutions provide an education that does not occur solely within the confines of either the classroom or the campus as it is traditionally defined. In explicitly rejecting the idea that the university must keep itself separate and cloistered from its surroundings, urban universities redefine the idea of place to include their urban neighbors. In doing so, they provide an increasingly critical alternative to the separatist philosophy that characterizes so many institutions of higher learning that embrace the collegiate ideal. In short, urban universities hold out the promise of providing the type of education that will prepare students to confront the difficulties inherent in the complex, multicultural world in which we live.

We believe that the mission embraced by urban universities creates an environment for intellectual inquiry and purposeful societal action that is equal to or superior to the notion of the "collegiate ideal." Indeed, the urban university model is ideally suited to confront the challenges faced by this country as we enter the twenty-first century. As Sheldon Hackney asserts, "For universities to stand aloof from the task of revitalizing our nation's schools and communities, when society has clearly decided that it is an urgent priority, simply will not be tolerated" (1994, p. 312). Urban universities have responded to this call to action by expanding the idea of place to encompass society in general, and the urban community in particular. It remains to be seen whether the remaining sectors of our system of higher education will do the same.

References

Adamany, D. "Sustaining University Values While Reinventing University Commitments to Our Cities." *Teachers College Record,* 1994, *95* (3), 324–331.

Elliott, P. G. *The Urban Campus: Educating the New Majority for the New Century.* Phoenix: The Oryx Press, 1994.

Estrada, L. F. "Anticipating the Demographic Future." *Change: The Magazine of Higher Learning.* May/June 1989, pp. 14–19.

Hackney, S. "Toward a University System for the Twenty-First Century." *Teachers College Record,* 1994, *95* (3), 311–316.

Lagemann, E. C. "Universities and Urban Life." *Teachers College Record,* 1994, *95* (3), 305–310.

O'Neill, J. M. "Temple Plots $800 Million in Projects." *The Philadelphia Inquirer,* January 25, 1998, B1, B7.

Riesman, D. "The Urban University." *Massachusetts Review,* 1967, *8,* 476–486.

Rhoads, R. A. *Freedom's Web: Student Activism in an Age of Cultural Diversity.* Baltimore, Md.: John Hopkins University Press, 1998.

"Temple Raises the Bar in Attempt to Attract Students from Suburbs." *The Philadelphia Inquirer,* Feb. 9, 1998, pp. A1 and A8.

Temple University School District of Philadelphia. *Partnership: Professional Development, School Cluster Jaymin S. Sanford.* Philadelphia, 1996.

U.S. Department of Commerce, Bureau of the Census. Number of Inhabitants, Part 1, United States Summary, Series PC80-1, A1:1-35. Washington, D.C.: U.S. Government Printing Office, 1990.

Veysey, L. R. *The Emergence of the American University.* Chicago: University of Chicago Press, 1965.

ERIN MCNAMARA HORVAT and KATHLEEN M. SHAW are assistant professors of higher education at Temple University.

Whatever forms they take, the colleges of the twenty-first century must incorporate educational fundamentals underlying traditional residential institutions.

The Collegiate Ideal in the Twenty-First Century

Arthur W. Chickering, Jackson Kytle

We need to recognize at the outset that the "ideal college" was just that, an ideal which carried lots of romance about students, learning, and collegiate life. The reality was more diverse, served more varied purposes, and many students fell short of the ideal. But despite its limitations, the ideal served at least two purposes: it motivated students and families to make the investment in higher education, and it recognized complex, living–learning interactions among all parts of academic life.

Sixty years of research documents the superior educational power of small, residential colleges. That research also documents the key ingredients that drive learning that lasts in those settings. According to Kytle, when the powerful parts of the collegiate ideal are working well, the involving college is the best institution yet invented for challenging and supporting students as they transform themselves into lifelong engaged learners and citizens (Kytle, 1999). But a wide range of current conditions are provoking new organizational structures, new modes of delivery, new curricular patterns, new mixes of teaching strategies. Some thoughtful observers predict that, thirty years from now, campus-based higher education will characterize only a small number of elite, highly selective, institutions. Others, paraphrasing Mark Twain, suggest that rumors of its demise are exaggerated. However accurate the prophecies, one thing is clear. When institutional purposes reach beyond basic information transfer and occupational or professional training, when they reach for broad-based cognitive and affective outcomes, these new forms will incorporate the underlying ingredients of educationally powerful residential colleges.

Research Findings

Several chapters in this volume (Kezar, Wolf-Wendel and Ruel, Amey, Ortiz) remind us of pertinent research and theory. One of the first, most comprehensive studies of commuting and resident students was carried out at the American Council on Education (ACE) Office of Research in 1970.

> Perhaps the most striking thing about these diverse studies is the consistency of the results. Whatever the institution, whatever the group, whatever the data, whatever the methods of analysis, the findings are the same. . . . Students who live at home, in comparison with those who live in college dormitories, are less fully involved in academic activities, in extracurricular activities, and in social activities with other students. Their degree aspirations diminish and they become less committed to a variety of long range goals. They enter educationally and developmentally useful experiences and activities less frequently. They report a shrinking range of competence. Their self-ratings for a diverse array of abilities and desirable personal characteristics drop. Their satisfaction with college decreases, and they become less likely to return [Chickering, 1974, pp. 84–85].

Twenty years later, Pascarella and Terenzini's comprehensive synthesis (1991) reported similar findings.

> Living on campus (versus commuting to college) is perhaps the single most consistent within-college determinant of impact. . . . Residential living is positively, if modestly, linked to increases in aesthetic, cultural, and intellectual values; a liberalizing of social, political, and religious values and attitudes; increases in self-concept, intellectual orientation, autonomy, and independence; gains in tolerance, empathy, and ability to relate to others; persistence in college; and bachelor's degree attainment [p. 610].

Findings like these prompted Alexander Astin's involvement theory (1985). That theory has encouraged subsequent research and action which amply demonstrate the superiority of the intensive, residential ideal for broad gauged learning and development of the whole person.

Current Challenges

Several authors recognize some of the powerful forces challenging traditional institutional forms. The challenges include:

- Changing student characteristics;
- More complex societal needs;
- Reduced support and pressures for accountability;
- Communication and information technologies; and
- Unclear purposes.

These forces are driving institutional restructuring, curricular changes, new orientations toward teaching and learning, increased efforts to assess complex outcomes, efforts to integrate academic studies and out-of-class experiences, and critical examination of faculty roles and responsibilities.

Changing Student Characteristics. The most powerful challenge to the collegiate ideal comes from changes in student characteristics. Kezar, Wolf-Wendel and Ruel, and Ortiz all address the problems and potentials flowing from increased diversity, shifting patterns of motivation, self-direction, financial need, lack of inclusion, and lack of sensitivity to cultural differences.

Until the early 1970s, the overwhelming majority of college students were white, between the ages of seventeen and twenty-two, middle and upper class in socioeconomic status. Now, the 1998 Almanac edition of *The Chronicle of Higher Education* reports that our students are 2.9 percent Asian, 9 percent Hispanic, and 12.1 percent Black; a significant proportion, 13.8 percent, speak a language other than English at home. In addition adult learners over the age of twenty-five, mostly women, became a significant constituency during the 1970s, reaching 38 percent by 1993. By 1998, *The Chronicle of Higher Education* Almanac reports 31.2 percent who are twenty-five to forty-four; 20.7 percent, forty-five to sixty-four; and 12.7 percent, sixty-five and older (pp. 5–7). About two-thirds of these students are working. More than half of the nation's college enrollees are attending part time.

This combination of characteristics means that fewer than one in six—some estimates say one in ten—of all undergraduates fits the traditional pattern of attending full time, being 18–22 years of age, and living on campus.

Levine and Cureton (1998) describe some of the implications.

> What this means is that higher education is not as central to the lives of today's undergraduates as it was to previous generations. Increasingly, college is just one of a multiplicity of activities in which they are engaged every day. For many, it is not even the most important of these activities; work and family often overshadow it.
>
> As a consequence, older, part time, and working students . . . want a different type of relationship with their colleges from the one undergraduates historically have had. . . . They want their colleges to be nearby and to operate at the hours most useful to them—preferably around the clock. They want convenience; easy, accessible parking (at the classroom door would not be bad); no lines; and a polite, helpful, efficient staff. They also want high-quality education but are eager for low costs. For the most part, they are willing to comparison shop, and they place a premium on time and money. They do not want to pay for activities and programs they do not use [p.14].

More Complex Societal Needs. These changing student characteristics reflect, in turn, changing social conditions and the more complex needs of a globally interdependent, multicultural, knowledge- and service-based society. Consider the requirements for an effective American work force identified by the American Society for Training and Development (ASTD), the professional association for persons employed in corporate education:

- Knowing how to learn;
- Competence in reading, writing, computation;
- Skills in listening and oral communication;
- Adaptability: creative thinking, problem solving;
- Personal management: self-esteem, goal setting, personal and career development;
- Group effectiveness: interpersonal skills, negotiating skills, teamwork; and
- Influence: organizational effectiveness, leadership.

Goodchild's historical overview and call for an integrative, humane view of collegiate purposes addresses these needs. So do Wolf-Wendell and Ruel when they argue for increased integration between academic and student affairs to deal with students as complex, whole persons. From a different perspective, Hagedorn recognizes the importance of integrating academic and vocational education, and the potential value of new technologies for achieving this integration.

If higher education does not generate educational outcomes consistent with those identified by ASTD and these authors, graduates may be prepared for jobs, but not for careers. Corporations, educational institutions, and human service organizations may get persons trained for entry level positions, but not hire employees prepared for more complex roles and responsibilities, able to handle changing workplace demands.

Today's society requires several levels of competence for career success, effective citizenship, a healthy marriage, generative parenting, and a satisfying life. These levels are interdependent. They involve not only cognitive complexity and interpersonal competence, but emotional intelligence, well grounded values, and a capacity to identify with something larger than individual self-interest. Higher education is the single, social institution capable of strengthening these competencies and personal characteristics throughout the population.

Reduced Support and Pressures for Accountability. During the 1980s and 1990s, funding, political support, and public respect for higher education have all declined. State legislators are raising questions about quality and productivity. Various performance funding programs link dollar allocations to evidence concerning general education outcomes, outcomes in majors, graduation rates, and the satisfaction and success of graduates. Loans are steadily replacing grants for financial aid. Faculty teaching loads are being scrutinized. Mass media criticize rising costs, mediocre student performance, redundancy and inefficiency.

Stanley Ikenberry (1998), in his recent "Letter from the President" to the American Council on Education Board, said:

We have witnessed a gradual but steady acceleration of national concern about the cost (or more accurately, the 'price') of higher education. . . . The public is completely convinced that college is important, but Americans fear it is not affordable for most families. . . . And most troubling, they don't believe colleges care [p. 4].

Levine (1997) suggests that these changes are not temporary.

American higher education has become a mature industry. More than 60 percent of all high school graduates are now going on to some form of post-secondary education. Increasingly, this is being viewed in the state capitals as sufficient or even as over-expansion of higher education. There is no enthusiasm by government for increasing the college attendance rate to 70 or 80 percent.

This represents a dramatic change in the attitude of government toward American higher education. . . . In the decades following World War II . . . Government's principal role was to expand higher education and increase opportunities for access. . . . Few questions were asked. This is the lot of growth industries in America.

Government treats mature industries very differently. It seeks to regulate or control them. It asks hard questions about their cost, efficiency, productivity, and effectiveness. It attempts to limit their size and funding. It reduces their autonomy, increases their regulation and demands greater accountability [pp. 4–5].

Communication and Information Technologies. Fast-changing, communication and information technologies powerfully interact with changing student characteristics, more complex societal needs, and reduced support. Kezar and Hagedorn recognize some of the problems and potentials associated with this major dynamic. These new tools may help (or they may not) if we take seriously the educational outcomes required for the twenty-first century. As yet, we have no general answers to questions like these:

Do computers teach better? There is huge contextual variability across educational purposes, content and competence categories, and pedagogies.

Do computers save money? Compared with what? We do not have good information about the cost effectiveness of current programs. What costs are included for using new technologies? Amortizing the infrastructure? Renovating facilities? Salaries, office space, and equipment for support staff? How do we take into account changing prices and changing capacities?

These new technologies raise hard questions for each institution. What is our mission? What outcomes for students do we value: knowledge acquisition, cognitive skills, interpersonal skills, group process skills, moral or ethical development, individual and social responsibility? All of the above?

What are our underlying assumptions about teaching; learning; evaluation; the role of professors, peers, other resource persons; the importance of classroom interactions; uses of experiential learning?

Decisions about new technologies are decisions about desired outcomes, about how learning occurs, and about pedagogical strategies. Investing in smart classrooms, presentation software and training, course-based didactic resources, evaluating individual mastery, and the model of the teacher as authority imply one set of assumptions. Strengthening communication capacity, using interactive software, training in identifying and using diverse resources, collaborative learning, and peer evaluation imply a quite different set of assumptions.

Kezar, Amey, and Horvat and Shaw address some of these issues. No college or university can ignore the potential of the new tools. They can be used in ways consistent with the educational values and principles embedded in the collegiate ideal as they try to cope with the powerful challenges they face. Or they can use them to batch process increasingly diverse students, delivering information, generating credits and credentials at lower costs, forfeiting the opportunity to strengthen our ability to meet complex, societal needs.

Unclear Purposes. Goodchild argues persuasively that today's colleges and universities lack clear purposes. Morphew's observations concerning the challenges to shared governance resulting from internal incoherence and from external pressures for greater efficiency are consistent with Goodchild's points. Horvat and Shaw's call for making urban universities an integral part of their environments instead of detached cloisters, using the city as classroom and laboratory, speaks to a similar issue.

Stanley Ikenberry agrees:

> Ultimately, the crucial challenge facing colleges and universities is not so much cost or technology, as profound as these may be, but the challenge of purpose: the demand to define and clarify why we exist; what it is we do best; what it is that we care about most. . . . If the purpose of the campus is the creation of a community of students and scholars who accomplish important things that are highly valued by the society, survival is not an issue. . . . If [higher education] has to do only with gaining access to information, acquiring employable skills, and gaining certification of competence, then campuses indeed are at risk [p. 5].

Key Ingredients of Educationally Powerful Environments

The ideal colleges of the twenty-first century will have to respond to these powerful societal forces. They will need to help students achieve the knowledge, competence, and personal characteristics required for career success, generative parenting and family relationships, and responsible citizenship. To generate such outcomes, they will need to create alternatives which embody fundamental educational conditions and processes that have characterized the ideal twentieth century college.

We know a good bit about the institutional characteristics which underlie that ideal when it is made real. *Involving Colleges* (Kuh, Schuh, Whitt, and

Associates, 1991), built on Astin's theory to "assess the contributions of out-of-class experiences to the overall quality of the undergraduate experience" in fourteen institutions. These colleges share five major ingredients: a clear mission, kept plainly in view; valuing and expecting student initiative and responsibility; recognizing and responding to the total student experience; providing small, human-scale environments and multiple sub-communities; valuing students and taking their learning seriously. This work, focusing on conditions and experiences outside the classroom, enriches other studies which examined variables concerning curriculum, pedagogy, and student-faculty relationships.

Chickering and Gamson (1987), with advice and counsel from a group of seasoned higher education professionals, posited seven principles consistent with prior research. Good practice in undergraduate education encourages student-faculty contact, encourages cooperation among students, encourages active learning, gives prompt feedback, emphasizes time on task, communicates high expectations, and respects diverse talents and ways of learning.

These principles and those cited in *Involving Colleges* are not only consistent with research concerning college impacts on student development, but are consistent with our growing understanding of human learning and development coming out of educational psychology and the cognitive sciences. Peter Ewell (1997), in an enormously useful synthesis, gave us "eight insights" from that literature.

> The learner is not a "receptacle" of knowledge but rather creates his or her learning actively and uniquely.
> Learning is about "meaning making" for an individual learner by establishing and reworking patterns, relationships, and connections.
> Every student can learn—and does learn all the time—with us or despite us.
> Direct individual experiences decisively shape individual understandings.
> Learning occurs when the learner is "ready" to learn.
> Learning occurs best in the context of a compelling "presenting problem."
> The results of learning atrophy if they are not exercised, while frequent feedback multiplies the already-strong learning effects of practice.
> Learning occurs best in a cultural and interpersonal context that supplies a great deal of enjoyable interaction and considerable levels of individual personal support [pp. 5–8].

Realizing the Ideal College in the Twenty-First Century

The ideal college of the twenty-first century will need policies and practices consistent with the Seven Principles and with Ewell's eight insights. What are some ways to be consistent with those while facing the challenges posed by changing student characteristics, complex societal needs, costs and accountability, new technologies, and confused purposes?

Clear Purposes. The bedrock requirement is clear purposes, the "crucial challenge" identified by Ikenberry. Internally consistent purposes are critically important for creating an educationally powerful culture of learning.

Research evidence dating back to Theodore Newcomb's 1938 studies of Bennington College indicates that clear, consistent institutional objectives make significant contributions to student development. In their comprehensive 1991 review of the literature, Pascarella and Terenzini say:

> The effects of specific within-college programs, conditions, or experiences consistently appear to be smaller than the overall net effects of the college. . . . The cumulative effect of all sub-environments—if they are mutually supportive—can be substantial. Thus, instead of singular, large, specially designed, and campuswide programs to achieve a particular institutional goal, efforts might more profitably focus on ways to embed the pursuit of that goal in all appropriate institutional activities [p. 610].

Unfortunately, in the 1980s Boyer (1987) found a pervasive absence of clear and consistent objectives.

> During our study we found divisions on campus, conflicting priorities and competing interests that diminish the intellectual and social quality of the undergraduate experiences and restrict the capacity of the college effectively to serve its students. At most colleges and universities we visited, these special points of tension appeared with such regularity and seemed so consistently to sap the vitality of the baccalaureate experience that we have made them the focus of this report [p. 2].

> Note that we are talking about educational purposes here, about desired outcomes in terms of student learning and personal development. Most catalogs make vague statements, but seldom are these purposes taken seriously and seldom are they sufficiently specific to drive decisions concerning institutional processes and practices. Alverno College is an outstanding exception. They have articulated eight abilities: Global Perspectives, Effective Citizenship, Aesthetic Responsiveness, Valuing in Decision Making, Communication, Problem Solving, Social Interaction, and Analysis. Most importantly, they have stated six levels of competence for each of these abilities and spelled out criteria for assessing each level. "To earn an Alverno degree, a student must demonstrate—along with a grasp of her discipline— mastery of these abilities at increasingly complex levels" [pp. 4–5].

Most institutions will not be up to this level of commitment to clear purposes because, in part, of the difficult work required to get the many interest groups in a college to agree on core outcomes. But until there are institutional commitments to clearly defined and agreed upon learning outcomes, conflicting priorities and competing interests will prevail. Once clear purposes are defined, then educational practices can be coordinated in their service. To be consistent with the best parts of the ideal college, these practices must:

Maximize human interactions among diverse learners and resource persons.
Employ pedagogies for active learning.
Recognize individual differences.
Integrate academic studies and experiential learning.
Set high expectations.

Maximizing Human Interactions. Past research documents that daily interactions with fellow students—in dormitories, in extracurricular activities, and in courses and classes—were the principal forces for student learning and development in the ideal college. Wolf-Wendel, Ruel, and Toma all speak to this point. Frequent interactions with faculty members, in relation to academic studies and in less formal contexts outside of class, ranked second. So, how do we generate analogous interactions for the twenty-first century college?

Intensive short-term residencies are one well-tested alternative. Brief residency programs bring students together for various time periods—ten days, two weeks, a month—every six months or so. These residencies immerse students in substantive perspectives, presentations, and feedback about their own products and performances, and systematic planning about learning contracts or learning plans to be pursued during the upcoming inter-residency period. Students meet with core faculty and with faculty whose professional expertise is pertinent to their program plans. Various types of formal and informal activities among students help build emotionally supportive and intellectually stimulating friendships. These residencies serve a very diverse mix of participants, coming from all parts of the United States and from other countries. Weekend residencies, typically occurring monthly or weekly, are another alternative. They provide a similar mix of interactions and serve a diverse mix of participants within a 150–200 mile radius.

Various resources for ongoing communication help sustain substantive interactions and emotional support between residencies. Until the 1990s, these interactions were primarily by mail, telephone, and conference calls. Now, new communication technologies boost the immediacy and richness through synchronous and asynchronous e-mail LISTSERVs, through various types of interactive software like Lotus LearningSpace and EMBAnet, and through institutional and individual Web pages.

The underlying purpose here is to create small "communities of commitment" (Kofman and Senge, 1995). Learning communities of the right psychological size treat participants as whole persons, not simply as minds to be filled or bodies to be trained. Brief intensive residencies do that.

Pedagogies for Active Learning. The dominant pedagogy in the ideal college was a lecture and a text, with mid-term and final exams. But there was a lot of informal active learning, through all night bull sessions in residence halls and through participation in academically oriented clubs and activities.

Now we need, and we are seeing, the emergence of pedagogies which enable those peer interactions. The new methods move from emphasizing didactic information transfer to stimulating analysis, synthesis, evaluation, and group problem solving. Note the new labels: problem-based learning, collaborative learning, case studies, dialogue, learning teams. Syllabi and course plans now include not only the sequence of content and reading assignments, but explicit designs for interactive processes during class sessions, and various kinds of active preparation between classes. In this volume, Kezar points us toward active learning strategies. Barr and Tagg (1995) give us an excellent basis for making this shift.

New technologies have powerful potential for strengthening active learning. They provide access to wide-ranging resources for learning: human expertise, libraries, and museums; virtual experiences of worldwide cities and towns, mountains, fields, and streams; day-to-day web-based follow-ups to news broadcasts and public interest programs; ongoing, topical discussion groups. And just as they can strengthen human interactions between intensive residencies, so too they can support learning teams, study groups, and peer evaluation.

Recognizing Individual Differences. The traditional ideal college served a relatively homogeneous clientele, mainly—with a few exceptions—upper middle class, white males. But that began to change following World War II with the G.I. Bill, which helped millions of veterans who otherwise could not have done so pursue higher education. Access and resulting student diversity were dramatically increased in the late 1960s by federal policy decisions that invested in student loans and grants instead of institutions. Those decisions moved higher education away from a "meritocratic orientation"—educating only the best and the brightest—to an "egalitarian orientation," making higher education accessible to everyone. This policy decision has enabled access to higher education for a wide range of students formerly excluded.

Population diversity will only increase. We know, for example, that Caucasians in California are going to make up less than fifty percent of the population by the year 2000. While we recognize not only the richness and opportunities provided by racial and ethnic diversity, educators have also become increasingly conscious of important differences in learning styles and developmental stages, motives, stamina, and multiple intelligences. Many students now expect consideration of their unique needs and differences in learning. Moreover, federal and state policies provide support for this change.

During the 1970s, there was a burst of energy and innovation responding to individual differences flowing from changing demographics. Many institutions created options for individualized degree programs with various approaches to individually designed courses, pursued through independent studies and learning contracts. Some new alternatives were located in new, freestanding institutions, while others were located in new colleges or programs within the larger host. Still others simply expanded the range of options within existing general education requirements or majors.

Those alternatives remain to be further developed and made available to a wider range of students. The new communication and information technologies increase dramatically our capacity to recognize and respond to differences in prior learning, in learning styles, in developmental stages, and in motivation. Faculty and staff development will be an important challenge if colleges are to respond to diverse students. Indeed, preparing students to understand and value diversity will be an essential learning outcome of the twenty-first century college, regardless of the form it takes.

Integrating Academic Studies and Experiential Learning. In the traditional ideal college, there was little explicit attention to experiential learning as we understand it today, nor were there any systematic attempts to integrate out-of-class experiences, on or off campus, with curricula, courses, or classes. Of course plenty of experiential learning went on—some for better, some for worse—in dormitories, in local bars, during weekend house parties and homecoming events, and through participation in diverse extracurricular activities. But there were no formal vehicles to help students reflect on those experiences, consider their implications for abstract concepts and theories, or to test academic ideas through active application.

Now we have ample evidence that creating opportunities for service learning, internships, field experiences, and relevant paid employment, and integrating these opportunities with academic studies, strengthens learning and influences significant dimensions of personal development. Adult learners are embedded in community activities and family responsibilities that provide experiential contexts relevant to many aspects of their studies. They, and most traditional college-age students, are employed in settings that also can provide experiential grist for academic mills. Creating more seamless webs between academic studies and wide-ranging opportunities for relevant experiences on and off campus will help colleges and universities respond to changing demographics, create more cost-effective education, and bolster learning that lasts. Colleges, especially complex colleges with specialized staff, might provide faculty and staff development that looks at the student as a whole person learning in a whole college environment.

Setting High Expectations. Quality education was assumed in the ideal college. The capacity of college graduates to perform on the job and as community leaders was unquestioned. Now legislators, parents, corporations, and community organizations voice concerns about the quality of higher education in relation to the competencies and personal characteristics required by a globally interdependent, multicultural information age.

These concerns collide with changing norms and assumptions among students about the levels of time, energy, and emotion required for learning. Time on task has become a serious problem. In the ideal college, the basic expectation called for two hours of preparation for every hour of class. Today in many institutions and for many students preparation time often does not equal class time; indeed, in some instances, no preparation can be assumed. Most full-time students are also working for more than a few hours. A recent survey at George Mason University, for example, found that 64 percent of students enrolled for twelve credits or more were also working more than twenty hours per week.

The ideal college of the twenty-first century will have to set clear and sound expectations for time on task and high standards of performance for broad outcomes to meet the needs for a competent work force, effective citizens, and generative parenting. To generate that performance, the whole college—administrators, faculty members, and student affairs professionals—will have to engage the whole student.

The foundation for the next generation of ideal colleges is establishing clear purposes and defining clear outcomes for student learning and personal development. But that foundation will serve little purpose if high expectations do not accompany the human interactions, individualization, and active, experiential learning which characterize programs and processes.

References

Astin, A. *Achieving Educational Excellence.* San Francisco: Jossey-Bass, 1985.

Barr, R. B., and Tagg, J. "From Teaching to Learning: A New Paradigm for Undergraduate Education." *Change,* 1995, 27 (6), 12–25.

Boyer, E. L. *College: The Undergraduate Experience in America.* New York: Harper and Row Publishers, 1987.

Chickering, A. W. *Commuting Versus Resident Students.* San Francisco: Jossey-Bass, 1974.

Chickering, A. W., and Gamson, Z. F. "Seven Principles for Good Practice in Undergraduate Education." *American Association of Higher Education Bulletin,* 1987, 39 (7), 3–7.

The Chronicle of Higher Education, Almanac Issue, 1988, 45 (1).

Ewell, P. T. "Organizing for Learning: A Point of Entry." Draft Prepared for Discussion at the AAHE Summer Academy at Snowbird, 1997.

Ikenberry, S. O. "Letter from the President." American Council on Education, Fall, 1998.

Kofman, F., and Senge, P. "Communities of Commitment." In S. Chawla and J. Renesch (eds.), *Learning Organizations.* Portland, Oreg.: Productivity Press, 1995.

Kuh, G. D., Schuh, J. H., Whitt, E. J., and Associates. *Involving Colleges: Successful Approaches to Fostering Student Learning and Development Outside the Classroom.* San Francisco: Jossey-Bass, 1991.

Kytle, J. "On Constructing an Engaged Life." In M. Miller and J. West (eds.), *Spirituality, Ethics, and Relationship.* International Universities Press: Madison, Conn., 1999.

Levine, A. "The State of American Higher Education." President's Essay, Teachers College, Columbia, *1997 Annual Report,* 4–16.

Levine, A., and Cureton, J. S. "Collegiate Life: An Obituary." *Change,* May/June, 1998, pp. 12–17.

"Liberal Arts at Alverno, Breaking Open the Patterns," *Alverno Magazine,* Milwaukee: Alverno College (Winter) 1997.

Pascarella, E. T., and Terenzini, P. T. *How College Affects Students: Findings and Insights From Twenty Years of Research.* San Francisco: Jossey-Bass, 1991.

ARTHUR W. CHICKERING *is visiting distinguished professor at Vermont College, Norwich University.*

JACKSON KYTLE *is vice president of Norwich University and Dean of Vermont College.*

INDEX

Achieving Educational Excellence (Astin), 42
Adamany, D., 103
Administrators, and shared governance, 71–78
Allmendinger, D. F., Jr., 12, 18
Alverno College, 19, 116
American Association of Community Colleges, 92
American Association of Higher Education, 61
American Association of University Professors (AAUP), 72, 74
American College and University, The (Rudolph), 9–10
American College Personnel Association, 36, 42
American Council on Education, 36, 110, 112
American Society for Training and Development (ASTD), 112
Americans, The (Boorstin), 8
Amey, M., 3, 5, 59, 110, 114
Amherst University, 17–18
Angelo, T. A., 61, 63, 64
Annis, L. F., 66
Antioch College, 19
Appleton, J. R., 36
Apps, J. W., 19
Assessment, of student learning, 64
Astin, A. W., 5, 20, 26, 27, 31, 37–38, 40, 42, 43, 50, 55, 110, 115
Athletics, 81–90
Atkinson, R. C., 60

Bailyn, B., 11, 12
Baldwin, R. G., 59
Baltzell, E. D., 13
Banta, T. W., 42
Barr, R. B., 63, 118
Batchelder, T., 29
Battisoni, R., 29
Bayer, A. E., 61
Bean, J. P., 26, 37
Belenky, M., 28, 29
Bennett, W. J., 41
Bennington College, 116
Berry, L., Jr., 29

Birnbaum, R., 73, 75, 78: collegiate model of, 73–75
Bloom, A., 41
Boschini, V. J., 51
Boorstin, D. J., 8, 9
Bowen, H. R., 35
Bowers, P. M., 27
Boyer, E. L., 20, 67, 116
Braxton, J. M., 61
Breck, A. D., 16
Briggs, C. M., 36
Brint, S., 18
Brubacher, J. S., 13–14, 16, 18, 73
Brufffee, K. A., 29
Bruhn, W., 27
Bryton, E., 93, 94, 95
Burack, C. A., 67
Burgess, J. W., 16–18
Burke, C. B., 12
Burton, J. D., 12
Butler, N. M., 17–18

California State University (CSU), 76
Campus culture: and collegiate ideal, 48–49; and nontraditional students, 55, 106; in urban universities, 101
Campus Life (Horowitz), 41
Carl D. Perkins Vocational and Applied Technology Act of 1990. See Perkins Act
Carnegie Foundation for the Advancement of Teaching, 16, 20–21
Carroll, S., 93, 94, 95
Carter, D., 27, 28
Chait, R., 40
Cheatham, H. E., 28
Chickering, A. W., 4–5, 31, 37, 39, 44, 47, 99, 110, 115
Chronicle of Higher Education, 40, 55, 111
Church, R. L., 13
Clark, B. R., 10
Clemson University, 87
Clinchy, B., 28, 29
College of William and Mary, 73
Colleges and universities: accountability of, 112–113; athletics at, 81–90; Birnbaum's model of, 73–75; and community relations, 101–106; core units of,

74; diversity at, 25–32; early development of, 11–20; environmental systems in, 77–78; human interactions in, 117; lack of purpose in, 114; nontraditional, 18–20; positive perceptions of, 85–88; residence halls in, 15; and societal needs, 111–112; technical systems in, 76–77; in urban settings, 101–106; women's, 15

Collegiate ideal: and athletics, 81–90; benefits of, 49–52; broadening of, 28–30; as campus culture, 48–49; challenges to, 110–114; characteristics of, 8; and development of students, 35–44; and diversity, 25–32; and elitism, 25; exporting of, 53–54; and faculty culture, 59–68; future of, 109–120; historical perspective of, 1, 8–11; and idea of place, 1–2, 92, 101–106; institutionalization of, 47–56; movement away from, 30–31; for nontraditional students, 54–56; and pluralism, 25–32; and shared governance, 71–78; six models of, 11–20; and student affairs, 52–54; transformations of, 7–21; and vocational education, 91–100

Collegiate way of learning, 14–16

Colonial way of learning, 11–12

Colorado Electronic Community College, 19–20

Columbia University, 17, 18

Community colleges: growth of, 18–19; vocational education at, 91–100

Community service learning (CSL), 29–30

Community way of learning, 18–19

Conant, J. B., 15–16

Continental America, 1800–1867 (Meinig), 8

Contract education, 96–97

Cowley, W. H., 12, 14, 18

Cremin, L. A., 8, 19

Cross, K. P., 61, 64

Cross, P. K., 31

Cureton, J., 25, 41, 111

Dartmouth College, 15

DePaul University, 19

Distance education, 19–20: drawbacks of, 30

Diversity: and collegiate ideal, 25–32; implications of, 31–32; of students, 26–28

Dressel, P. L., 16

D'Souza, D., 41

Duke University, 87

Dukerich, J. M., 83

Dutton, J. E., 83

Edgerton, R., 66

Eimers, M. T., 61

Elazar, D. J., 8

Electronic University Network, 19

Elitism, 25

Elliott, P. G., 103

Empire State College, 19

Epper, R. M., 19

Epstein, P., 98

Erikson, E., 51

Estrada, L. F., 103

Evergreen State College, 19

Ewell, P. T., 115

Experimental College (University of Wisconsin), 7

Faculty: changing role of, 64–65; pressures on, 59–60; and research, 67; reshaping incentives of, 59–68; service of, 67–68; and shared governance, 71–78; and teaching, 66–67

Fairweather, J. S., 60

Feldman, K. A., 27, 47, 66

Finkelstein, M., 12

Fletcher, R. S., 13

Flexner, A., 15

Frederiksen, C. F., 16

Freeman, J., 18

Fretwell, E. K., 44

Frontier way of learning, 12–14

Fundraising, and athletics, 85

Gamson, Z. F., 115

Gates, S., 93

Geiger, R. L., 13

Geltner, B. B., 29

Geoghegan, W. H., 63

George Mason University, 118–119

Goddard College, 19

Goldberger, N., 28, 29

Goodchild, L. F., 2, 5, 8, 10, 15, 19, 114

Goodsell, A. G., 29

Gorman, M., 30

Gosman, E. J., 27

Grant, G., 16, 19

Grubb, W. N., 91

Hackney, S., 103, 106

Hagedorn, L. S., 4, 113

Hampshire College, 19
Hall, J. D., 49
Hall, P., 30
Hall, S., 30
Hardy, C. M., 51
Harquail, C. V., 83
Harrison, A. W., 83
Harvard University: faculty discontent at, 73; founding of, 11–12; residence halls at, 15
Heyl, B. S., 29
Higher Education Facilities Act of 1963, 16
Higher Education Research Institute (HERI), 40, 41
Hirsch, D. J., 68
Homecoming, 84–85
Horowitz, H. L., 41
Horvat, E. M., 4, 114
Houle, C. O., 19
Human development, theory of, 37
Hurt, R. D., 12, 13
Hurtado, S., 27, 28
Hutchings, P., 66
Hutchins, R. M., 102

Ikenberry, S. O., 112, 114, 116
Ingelbret, E., 43
Integration theory, 38
Intercollegiate athletics. See Athletics
Internet education: drawbacks of, 30–31; growth of 19–20. See also On-line communities; Technology
Involvement theory, 26, 37–38, 110
Involving Colleges (Kuh, Schuh, Whitt, and Associates), 43, 49, 114–115
Irvine, L., 30

Jacob, P., 15
Jacobs, B. A., 51
Jacoby, B., 20, 29
Jencks, C., 18, 19
Johnson, E. L., 14
Joliet Junior College (Illinois), 18
John F. Kennedy University, 19
Johnson, D. W., 31
Johnson, R. T., 31
Jones Intercable, 19
Junior colleges. See Community colleges

Kaldor Criterion, 98
Kanoy, K. W., 27
Karabel, J., 18
Keeton, M. T., 16

Kelley, H. E., 44
Kett, J. F., 19
Kezar, A. J., 2, 5, 27, 110, 111, 113, 114, 118
Kirkpatrick, J. E., 15, 18
Kofman, F., 117
Kuh, G. D., 5, 20, 26, 27, 31, 42, 43, 49, 61, 114
Kytle, J., 4–5, 99, 109

Lagemann, E. C., 101, 102
Lawlis, C. L., 11
Learning: collaborative, 28–29; faculty focus on, 61–63; and peer groups, 27; and technology, 30–31
Learning College for the Twenty-First Century, A (O'Banion), 62
Learning communities, 29, 63
Leatherman, C., 78
Leslie, D. W., 44
Leslie, W. B., 13, 14
Levine, A., 25, 41, 111, 113
Levine, D. O., 18
Levine, J., 29
Liberal College, The (Meikeljohn), 7
Louisiana State University, 84, 86
Love, P. G., 51
Lucas, C. J., 35, 73
Luce, J., 30
Lynch, A. Q., 44

Mable, P., 16, 27
Mael, F. A., 83
Magner, D. K., 77
Manning, K., 49
Masden, G. M., 13
Martin, W. B., 10
Mattering, 44
Maylath, B., 28
McGregory, J., 31
Meiklejohn, A., 7, 20
Meinig, D. W., 8–9, 11, 13
Metzner, B. S., 26, 37
Meyer, J. W., 75
Mercer University, 15
Menges, R. J., 61, 62
Michigan State University, 16, 84
Miller, G. J., 98
Miller, M. T., 50
Miller, P., 11
Mills, M. K., 97, 98
Mind Extension University, 19
Minnesota Metropolitan University, 19

Moore, K. M., 12, 59
Morgan, J., 12
Morgan State College, 19
Morison, S. E., 11
Morphew, C. C., 3, 77, 114
Mount Holyoke College, 15

Nagel, S. S., 97, 98
National Association of Student Personnel Administrators, 36
National Center for Education Statistics, 77
National Defense Education Act of 1958, 16
National Society for Experiential Education (NSEE), 30
National Technological University, 19
Nettles, M. T., 27
New England Mind, The (Miller), 11
Newcomb, T., 27, 47, 116
Newcombe, T. M., 20
Newman, R. E., 50
Northwestern University, 85, 86

O'Banion, T., 62, 63, 64, 65, 66
Oberlin College, 13
O'Donnell, J. L., 30, 56
Ohio Frontier, The (Hurt), 12
O'Neill, J. M., 106
On-line communities, 63–64. See also Distance education; Internet education; Technology
Ortiz, A., 3, 5, 110, 111

Pascarella, E. T., 38, 110, 116
Paulsen, M. B., 66
Pavel, D. M., 43
Perkins Act, 92, 93, 100
Perry, W., 47
Pfeffer, J., 75
Pfnister, A. O., 14
Philadelphia Inquirer, 106
Place, idea of: and urban universities, 101–106; and vocational education, 92
Pluralism, 25–32
Potts, D. B., 8, 9, 13
Presbyterian colleges, 13
Priestly, W. J., 31
Princeton University, 14, 15
Principles of Good Practice for Student Affairs, 36–37
Public Law 101-392. See Perkins Act

Quinlan, K., 66

Ratcliff, J. L., 26
Rau, W., 29
Regis University, 20
Reinert. SJ, P. C., 10, 16
Reisser, L., 31, 37
Research, of faculty, 67
Residence halls: early development of, 15; funding for, 16
Rhatigan, J. J., 36
Rhoads, R., 104
Riesman, D., 16, 18, 19, 101
Rohrbough, M. J., 8
Root, S., 29
Rowan, B., 75
Rudolph, F., 9–10, 11, 13, 14, 15, 18, 35, 73, 93
Rudy, W., 13–14, 16, 18, 73
Ruel, M., 2, 5, 110, 111, 112
Ruppert, S., 98
Russo, P., 29

Salancik, G., 75
Sandman, L., 68
Sanford, N., 16, 51
Schein, H. K., 27
Schlossberg, N. K., 44
Schmidt, G. P., 16
Schroeder, C. C., 16, 27
Schuh, J. H., 5, 20, 43, 49, 114
Schultz, J., 30
Seagren, A. T., 50
Sedlak, M. W., 13
Seelye, J. H., 17
Selldin, P., 66
Senge, P., 117
Service, of faculty, 67–68
Shaping of America, The (Meinig), 8
Shared governance, 71–78: and Birnbaum's college model, 73–75; and environmental systems changes, 77–78; historical perspective of, 73; and technical system changes, 75–76
Shaw, K., 4, 114
Silva, E., 77
Singleton, S. E., 68
Slaughter, S., 77
Smith, B. L., 29
Smith, D., 31, 32
Smith, K. A., 31
Smith, T. B., 26, 27
Smith College, 15
Solomon, B. M., 15
Stage, F. K., 37

Stanton, G. C., 30
Stinson, S., 27
Stone, A., 93
Student affairs: establishment of, 47–56; institutionalization of collegiate ideal through, 52–54; and student development, 35–36, 37
Student Learning Imperative, The (American College Personnel Association), 42
Students: benefits of collegiate environment for, 26–28, 49–52; characteristics of, 39–40, 111; demographics of, 40–41; development of, 35–44; diversity of, 25–32, 40, 118; and faculty guidance, 27; minority, 26–27; nontraditional, 54–56, 92; peer groups among, 27; problems of, 40–41; psychological needs of, 51; satisfaction of, 27; traditional, 50–51; in vocational education, 92
Students Helping In the Naturalization of Elders (SHINE), 104
Susman, M. B., 20
Sutton, C. D., 83

Tagg, J., 63, 118
Tarule, J., 28, 29
Teaching, faculty responsibilty for, 66–67
Technology: changes in, 75–76; drawbacks of, 30–31; future issues in, 113–114; and human interactions, 117; as threat to idea of place, 93–94. *See also* Distance education; Internet education; On-line communities
Temple University, 103–106
Terenzini, P. T., 26, 27, 38, 110, 116
Tetrick, L. E., 83
Thoeney, A. R., 27
Thomas A. Edison State College, 19
Tierney, W. G., 38
Tinto, V., 29, 38–39, 40, 49, 50
Tolbert, P. S., 75
Toma, J. D., 4, 5
Tompkins, D., 29
Town way of learning, 16–18

Transformation of the School, The (Cremin), 8
Triesman, U., 27
Truman Report on Higher Edcation, 19
Tulane University, 87
Tuzin, D., 60

U.S. Department of Commerce, 102
U.S. Department of Education, 92, 95
University of California, Santa Cruz, 16
University of Chicago, 15, 87, 102
University of Connecticut, 87
University of Kansas, 39
University of Maryland, 20
University of Michigan, 13, 27, 84, 86, 87
University of Minnesota, 19
University of Nebraska, 82–83, 87, 89
University of Nevada at Las Vegas, 85
University of Virginia, 13

Van De Hende, M., 43
Vassar College, 15, 41
Veysey, L. R., 41, 102
Vocational education, 91–100: and contract education, 96–97; definition of, 92; fiscal restraints in, 93–96; superoptimum solutions for, 97–99

Wade, R. C., 9
Warren, K., 30
Webb, C. H., 50
Wellesley College, 15
Wertenbaker, T. J., 14
Western Governors University, 20, 63
Western Interstate Commission for Higher Education, 20
Whitt, E. J., 5, 20, 43, 49, 114
Wolf-Wendel, L., 2, 5, 43, 110, 111, 112
Woodson, J., 27

Yale University, 15
Young, J. R., 76

Zubizarreta, J., 66

Back Issue/Subscription Order Form

Copy or detach and send to:

Jossey-Bass Inc., Publishers, 350 Sansome Street, San Francisco CA 94104-1342

Call or fax toll free!

Phone 888-378-2537 6AM-5PM PST; Fax 800-605-2665

Back issues: Please send me the following issues at $23 each.

(Important: please include series initials and issue number, such as HE90.)

1. HE _____

_____

_____

$ _____ Total for single issues

$ _____ Shipping charges (for single issues *only;* subscriptions are exempt from shipping charges): Up to $30, add $5^{50} • $30^{01}–$50, add $6^{50} $50^{01}–$75, add $7^{50} • $75^{01}–$100, add $9 • $100^{01}–$150, add $10 Over $150, call for shipping charge.

Subscriptions   Please ❏ start ❏ renew my subscription to *New Directions for Higher Education* for the year 19___ at the following rate:

❏ Individual $56   ❏ Institutional $99

NOTE: Subscriptions are quarterly, and are for the calendar year only. Subscriptions begin with the spring issue of the year indicated above. For shipping outside the U.S., please add $25.

$ _____ Total single issues and subscriptions (CA, IN, NJ, NY and DC residents, add sales tax for single issues. NY and DC residents must include shipping charges when calculating sales tax. NY and Canadian residents only, add sales tax for subscriptions.)

❏ Payment enclosed (U.S. check or money order only)

❏ VISA, MC, AmEx, Discover Card #_____ Exp. date_____

Signature _____ Day phone _____

❏ Bill me (U.S. institutional orders only. Purchase order required.)

Purchase order #_____

Name _____

Address _____

_____

_____

Phone_____ E-mail _____

For more information about Jossey-Bass Publishers, visit our Web site at: www.josseybass.com   **PRIORITY CODE = ND1**

OTHER TITLES AVAILABLE IN THE
NEW DIRECTIONS FOR HIGHER EDUCATION SERIES
Martin Kramer, Editor-in-Chief

HE104 The Growing Use of Part-Time Faculty: Understanding Causes and Effects,
       David W. Leslie
HE103 Enhancing Productivity: Administrative, Instructional, and Technological
       Strategies, *James E. Groccia, Judith E. Miller*
HE102 Minority-Serving Institutions: Distinct Purposes, Common Goals,
       Jamie P. Merisotis, Colleen T. O'Brien
HE101 The Experience of Being in Graduate School: An Exploration, *Melissa S. Anderson*
HE100 The Campus-Level Impact of Assessment: Progress, Problems, and Possibili-
       ties, *Peter J. Gray, Trudy W. Banta*
HE99   Rethinking the Dissertation Process: Tackling Personal and Institutional Obsta-
       cles, *Lester F. Goodchild, Kathy E. Green, Elinor L. Katz, Raymond C. Kluever*
HE98   The Professional School Dean: Meeting the Leadership Challenges,
       Michael J. Austin, Frederick L. Ahearn, Richard A. English
HE97   The University's Role in Economic Development: From Research to Outreach,
       James P. Pappas
HE96   Preparing Competent College Graduates: Setting New and Higher Expecta-
       tions for Student Learning, *Elizabeth A. Jones*
HE95   An Administrator's Guide for Responding to Campus Crime: From Prevention
       to Liability, *Richard Fossey, Michael Clay Smith*
HE94   Strategies for Promoting Excellence in a Time of Scarce Resources,
       David W. Breneman, Alton L. Taylor
HE93   Leadership Transitions: The New College President, *Judith Block McLaughlin*
HE92   Conflict Management in Higher Education, *Susan A. Holton*
HE91   Assessing Performance in an Age of Accountability: Case Studies,
       Gerald H. Gaither
HE90   Information Technology and the Remaking of the University Library,
       Beverly P. Lynch
HE89   Rethinking Tuition and Student Aid Strategies, *Edward P. St. John*
HE88   Academic Freedom: An Everyday Concern, *Ernst Benjamin, Donald R. Wagner*
HE87   Developing Administrative Excellence: Creating a Culture of Leadership,
       Sharon A. McDade, Phyllis H. Lewis
HE86   Total Quality Management on Campus: Is It Worth Doing? *Daniel Seymour*
HE85   America's Investment in Liberal Education, *David H. Finifter, Arthur M. Hauptman*
HE84   Strengthening the College Major, *Carol Geary Schneider, William Scott Green*
HE83   Financial Management: Progress and Challenges, *William E. Vandament,
       Dennis P. Jones*
HE82   Important Lessons from Innovative Colleges and Universities, *V. Ray Cardozier*
HE81   Recognizing Faculty Work: Reward Systems for the Year 2000,
       Robert M. Diamond, Bronwyn E. Adam
HE80   Assessment and Curriculum Reform, *James L. Ratcliff*
HE79   Agendas for Church-Related Colleges and Universities, *David S. Guthrie,
       Richard L. Noftzger, Jr.*
HE78   Information Literacy: Developing Students as Independent Learners,
       D. W. Farmer, Terrence F. Mech
HE77   The Campus and Environmental Responsibility, *David J. Eagan, David W. Orr*
HE76   Administration as a Profession, *Jonathan D. Fife, Lester F. Goodchild*
HE75   Faculty in Governance: The Role of Senates and Joint Committees in
       Academic Decision Making, *Robert Birnbaum*
HE74   The Changing Dimensions of Student Aid, *Jamie P. Merisotis*
HE73   Using Consultants Successfully, *Jon F. Wergin*
HE72   Administrative Careers and the Marketplace, *Kathryn M. Moore, Susan B. Twombly*
HE70   An Agenda for the New Decade, *Larry W. Jones, Franz A. Nowotny*

HE69   Financial Planning Under Economic Uncertainty, *Richard E. Anderson,*
       Joel W. Meyerson
HE67   Achieving Assessment Goals Using Evaluation Techniques, *Peter J. Gray*
HE64   Successful Strategic Planning: Case Studies, *Douglas W. Steeples*
HE62   Making Computers Work for Administrators, *Kenneth C. Green, Steven W. Gilbert*
HE61   Leaders on Leadership: The College Presidency, *James L. Fisher, Martha W. Tack*
HE60   Increasing Retention: Academic and Student Affairs Administrators in
       Partnership, *Martha McGinty Stodt, William M. Klepper*
HE59   Student Outcomes Assessment: What Institutions Stand to Gain, *Diane F. Halpern*